The Complete HEART HEALTHY Cookbook For Women Over 50

1500 Days of Tasty Low-Sodium & Low-Fat Recipes to Stop Hypertension, Low Cholesterol, Keep Weight Under Controll with Easy-to-Find Ingredients

Elena Barba

The Complete Heart Healthy Cookbook for Women Over 50 2023 © Elena Barba

All rights reserved.

Release Date: Febb 2023

No part of this publication may be reproduced, distributed, or transmitted in any form or by any means, including photocopying, recording, or other electronic or mechanical methods, without the prior written permission of the publisher, except in the case of brief quotations embodied in critical reviews and certain other noncommercial uses permitted by copyright law.

Please note that the informations contained within this document is for educational and entertainment purpose only. All effort has been executed to present accurate, up to date, reliable, complete informations.

The author is not engaged in rendering professional advice to the reader. Suggestions contained in this book are not intended as a substitute for consulting with your physician. Your health require medical supervision. The author shall not be responsible for any damage arising from informations or suggestions in this book.

No warranties of any kind are declared or implied. Readers acknowledge that the author is not engaged in the rendering of legal, financial, medical or professional advice.

By reading this document, the reader agrees that under no circumstances is the author responsible for any losses, direct or indirect, that are incurred as a result of the use of the information contained within this document, including, but not limited to, errors, omissions.

Dedicated to all women over 50, like me, who want to start a healthier new life.

Menopause causes great changes in our body.

We have weight increase, hypertension and much more bad cholesterol in our blood.

Body and mind stress, overweight, fluid retention, high blood pressure can take us rapidly to a heart disease.

Men and women body are different, diet and lifestyle must be different too.

Modest lifestyle changes reduces cardiovascular disease.

Having a Heart Healthy Diet works to low cholesterol and blood pressure, gives more energy to body, let you lose weight, decreases fluid retention.

What are we waiting for?

Summary

High Blood Pressure and Women over 50 — 9

High Bad Cholesterol and Women Over 50 — 9

Heart diseases and Risk Factors — 10

A Heart Healthy Diet for Women Over 50 — 11

How to Make Heart Healthy Meals — 15

Kitchen Conversion Tables — 16

5 Weeks Meal Plans — 17

Low-Sodium Low-Fat Snacks — 24

- Celery Sticks with Cream Cheese Mousse — 25
- Oatmeal Almonds and Blueberries Granola Bar — 25
- Lemon Pepper Roasted Chickpeas — 25
- Tzatziki Dip — 25
- Peanut Butter Hummus — 26
- Crunchy Veggie Chips — 26
- Vanilla Yogurt with Peach and Pear — 26
- Vanilla Yogurt with Walnut and Apple — 27
- Low-Fat Chicken Empanadas — 27
- Lemon & Ricotta Italian Frittelle — 28
- Choccolate-Dipped Frozen Banana — 28
- Edamame Guacamole — 28
- Easy British Dried Fruit Flapjacks — 29

Low-Sodium Low-Fat Breakfast — 30

- Healthy Banana Nut Pancakes — 31
- French Toast with Strawberries — 31
- Apple-Pie Bread — 31
- Avocado Banana Smoothie — 32
- Banana Oats Muffins — 32
- Chocolate and Orange Muffins — 32
- Rice Pudding with Blueberries and Figs — 33
- Orange Low-Fat Yogurt Muffin — 34
- Cranberry Bliss Bars — 34
- Cherry and Pistachio Yogurt Parfait — 35
- Apple Crisp Recipe — 35
- Strawberry Almond Chia Pudding — 35
- Toast with Ricotta Cheese and Sun-Dried Tomatoes — 36
- Breakfast Burrito Recipe — 36
- Berry Cheesecake Parfait — 36
- Pumpkin Banana Bread Baked Oatmeal — 37
- Homemade Super Easy Oatmeal Cookies — 37
- Starbucks Pumpkin Scones Copycat Recipe — 38
- Light Oats Wholemeal Cookies — 39

Low-Sodium Low-Fat Doughs — 40

- Whole wheat tortillas — 40
- Bamboo Piadina — 40
- Ricotta bread rolls — 41
- Almond flour bread rolls — 41
- Rice Flour Shortbread Dough (gluten-free/ no butter) — 41
- Homemade Olive Oil Phyllo dough — 41
- Pie Crust Dough Recipe -double 9-inch pie pan recipe — 41
- Easy Flaky Oil Pie Crust (for sweet and savory fillings) — 42

Olive Oil Tart Crust 9-inch pie pan recipe	42
Italian Homemade Family Wholemeal Pizza Dough	43

Low-Sodium Homemade Seasonings — 44

Taco Seasoning Spices Mix	44
Garam Masala Homemade Mix	44
Jamaican Jerk Seasoning Mix	44
Steak Seasoning Mix	44
Fajita Seasoning Mix	44

Low-Sodium Low-Fat Soups — 45

Tuscany "Ribollita" italian recipe	45
Harvest Pumpkin Soup	46
Creamy Mushroom Soup	46
Chunky Vegetable Lentil Soup	46
Curried Mushrooms and Cauliflower Soup	47
Beef and Barley Soup	47
Broccoli Cheese Soup	48
Stuffed Pepper Soup	48
Turkey Long Grain Rice Soup	48
Dairy-Free Chicken Pot Pie Soup	49

Low-Sodium Low-Fat Pasta — 50

Healthy Shrimps Spaghetti Italian Style	50
Catfish & Cherry Tomatoes Pasta	51
Sicilian Ricotta & Pistachios Penne Rigate	51
Orecchiette Pasta with Broccoli Florets	51
Creamy Zucchini Sauce Fusilli	52
Chicken & Black Kale Pasta Skillet	52
Cauliflower & Peas Pasta	52
Lentil & Celery Ditalini Pasta	53
Tomato & Basil Caprese Pasta Salad	53
Fresh Salmon Fettuccine Skillet	54
Red Bell Pepper Macaroni	55
Walnuts & Basil Penne	55
Spinach & Ricotta Spaghetti	55
One-Pot Meat Sauce Pasta Recipe	56
Eggplant & Ricotta Rigatoni	56
Artichokes and black olives Fettuccine	57

Low-Sodium Low-Fat Vegetables and Salads — 58

Tomatoes & Cucumber Salad	58
Salmon Salad with Orange Vinaigrette	58
Green Salad with Beets and Edamame	58
Red and Yellow Bell Peppers with Zucchini	58
Lemon Chickpeas Quinoa Salad	59
Eggplants & Tomatoes Skillet Italian-Style	60
Summer Greens with Apple and Almonds	60
Sweet Potatoes Lentil Salad	60
Healthy Sauteed Cabbage	61
Sweet Potatoes and Kale Salad	61
Beetroot Cutlets	62
Southwestern Beans Salad	62
Glazed Carrost and Sweet Potatoes Salad	62
Baked Zucchini and Potatoes Sticks	62
Veggie Potato Gateau	63
Tuscany Panzanella Salad	63

Low-Sodium Low-Fat Meat — 64

Healthy Veggie Family Meatloaf 64
Baked Turkey Meatballs 65
Easy Baked Boneless Chicken Thighs 65
Orange Chicken Cutlets 65
Healthy Pepper Chicken Fajitas 65
Creamy Tofu and Turkey Salad 66
Sweet Potato & Peas Lamb Chops 66
Homemade Ground Turkey Burgers 66
Easy Grilled Pineapple Chicken 67
Mediterranean Grilled Chicken 67
Italian Marinara Meatballs 68
Easy Mexican Taco Turkey Meatloaf 68
Yummy Creamy Spinach Turkey Skillet 68
Orange and Onion Chicken 69
Spinach & Chickpeas Lemon-spiced Chicken 69
Pepper & Broccoli Chicken Pan 69

Low-Sodium Low-Fat Seafood 70

Easy Honey Garlic Salmon 70
Lemon Baked Cod 70
Spiced Tilapia with Tomatoes 70
Parsley Lime Halibut Fillets 70
Pepper Crusted Ahi Tuna & Arugula Salad 71
Broiled Garlic Tilapia & Grenn Beans 71
Flounder Fillets & Black Olive Tomato Sauce 72
Blackened Cod & Tomato Basil Salade 73
Florentine Sea Bass & Creamy Spinach 73
Tuna & Avocado Salad 73
Grilled Snapper in Orange Sauce 74
Baked Tilapia with Garlic and Herbs 74
Crispy Lemon Sea Bass 74
Grilled Tandoori Catfish 75
Anchovies Marinated in Vinegar 75

Low-Sodium Low-Fat Savory Pies & Pizza 76

Spanakopita: a Greek Savory Pie 76
Fresh Zucchini Pie 76
Creamy Tomato Pie 76
Yummy Focaccia Pizza Margherita 77
Creamy Broccoli and Ricotta Pie 77

Low-Sodium Low-Fat Desserts 78

Low Fat Homemade Vanilla Ice Cream 78
Healthy Pistachio and Date Raw Bites 78
Coconut Banana Ice Cream 79
BlackBerries Rice Pudding 79
Low Fat & Low Sodium Apple Pie 79
Low Fat Hazelnut and Pear Flan 80
Dairy-Free Iced Mocha Latte 80
Dark Chocolate Pistachio Fudge Balls 80
Black Bean Brownies 81
Super Easy Vanilla Banana Mug Cake 82
Almon Vanilla Fruit Salad 82
Low Fat Carrot Almond Cake 82
Low Fat Yummy Strawberry Shortcake 83

Index 84

High Blood Pressure and Women over 50

Hypertension, or high blood pressure, develops when blood flows at higher than normal pressure through vessels.

Men and women of all ages can be affected with hypertension and this can frequently cause severe health problems.

We all have to work to have it under control, but women over 50 should be particularly mindful of their numbers.

Controlling blood pressure can help in preventing damage to the heart, blood vessels, eyes, kidneys and also the brain. Nobody is too young to control blood pressure, but the risk of hypertension is higher as you are postmenopausal. Also during pregnancy, women must have extra care in controlling blood pressure.

You don't need any extreme signal to do your control, but considering that low energy, sleeping problems, hot flashes, chest pain and fluid retention are warning signs, if you have one of them please make a pressure control. To low high blood pressure it's important to reduce your intake of sodium.

Studies such as "The Dietary Approaches to Stop Hypertension" show that reducing sodium income to 1.500 mg a day can help to control blood pressure. Sodium is not just salt. Most of the sodium you take is in processed food you buy in markets or stores. Learning to read food labels is your first step to start controlling your sodium income.

How to Check Blood Pressure

Checking Blood pressure:

- Don't smoke, exercise or take caffeine, at least 30 minutes before.
- Relax and sit on a chair near a table.
- Harm must be at the same level as heart. Don't talk.

High Bad Cholesterol and Women Over 50

High Bad Cholesterol in the blood it's a serious condition that raises heart disease risks.

There are two types of cholesterol: LDL (Low-Density Lipoprotein) the "bad one", which carries cholesterol to arteries and tissues, and HDL (High-Density Lipoprotein) the "good one", which takes bad cholesterol from tissues and arteries and brings it to the liver, who works to remove it. If LDL is more than HDL, bad cholesterol is trapped in vessels and, over time, builds up plaques on their walls. Vessels narrow and harden and blood doesn't circulate well, becoming unable to bring oxygen and nutrients to the body and heart.

This process can happen anywhere in your body, but when affecting coronary arteries (coronary heart disease) it can cause angina or chest pain. Sometimes it can cause blood clots, blocking blood flowing and causing a heart attack.

Coronary heart disease is the most dangerous heart disease, and, together with other risk factors, increases the chance of developing a serious heart problem.

Saturated fat increases bad cholesterol more than anything else.

Food with soluble fiber helps to lower blood cholesterol. Soluble fibers mix with liquid, bind fat, and take it out of the body. Fruits, vegetables, cereal grains and vegetables have soluble fibers.

A heart-healthy diet for women over 50 must be a well-balanced eating plan, with a good balance of all the nutrients your body need.

Factors causing unhealthy cholesterol levels

Out of your control:

- Heredity (familiar genes, family history)
- Sex and Age. For women over 50 LDL level rises more than for men, because of menopause.

Under your control:

- Diet. Saturated fat, trans fat and cholesterol from animal products increase your LDL level more than all other elements of your diet.
- Overweight. It increases your LDL level and raises triglycerides.
- Physical activity. Physical inactivity leads to increase weight and LDL levels.
- Lifestyle: Smoking, alcohol intake.

Heart diseases and Risk Factors

Heart disease is a general term that includes many types of heart problems. Cardiovascular disease, which affects the heart and blood vessels, is the most common. Artery walls get thickened with fats standing on them and blood doesn't flow well. In this case heart has to work harder with increased risks of heart attack or stroke.

Apart from a cardiovascular disease family history, there are other important things to consider such as smoking, physical activity, stress and obesity, as said in the previous page, when considering risk factors.

Being overweight increases your possibility to develop diabetes, high blood pressure, and high cholesterol.

To live healthy and reduce your risks consider taking care of your body and follow these simple advice.

- Eat a Heart Healthy Diet, have low sodium, low saturated fats meal plans, with more fresh vegetables and fruits and whole grains.

- Lose weight. Obesity is dangerous for blood pressure. Changing your diet will give great benefits. Ask your family to help you with the grocery list and the cooking time..

- Be physically active; 2/3 hours of weekly physical activity or 20/30 minutes every day. Move more, a simple morning walk can make you feel better. The key to success is starting slowly and gradually increasing your effort.

- Stop smoking and vaping. Tobacco and nicotine are your enemies. Smoking damages your blood vessels and your heart.

- Sleep 7/8 hours for nights. Sleeping well and for a good time has an important role in relaxing the mind and body.

A Heart Healthy Diet for Women Over 50

There are no secret ingredients to cook a heart-healthy diet. You just have to cook meals with low saturated fat, low trans fat and low sodium food. Dishes must have fewer calories than those higher in fats. As we have seen women's body is not like men's. Researches and studies prove that we have different needs and, after menopause, differences between the body and health of men and women increase.

Menopause causes a lot of physical ailments, fluid retention, body and mind stress, irritability, high blood pressure, and fat accumulation in the abdominal area. The calorie requirement is lowered. Ovaries decrease estrogen production and this increases cardiovascular risk and osteoarticular pathologies, in particular the increase in the incidence of osteoporosis.

After menopause we have to keep under control nutrients like Calcium, vitamin D, magnesium, and vitamin K, as well as zinc, selenium, and vitamins E, C, and B6.

How is it possible to have a unique diet plan working well, at the same time, for men and women if our needs are so different?

As a general rule, a Heart Healthy diet must consider a plan with fresh fruit and vegetables, whole grain, vegetable protein, a few animal proteins, fat-free dairy, and low-sodium and low-fat content food. But, as needs are different, women have to have a daily income of about 1500/1800 calories, it depends on physical activity, and men 2000/2200 calories. Women must keep off saturated fats and choose fat-free products because menopause raises LDL levels. Men do have not this problem at all. Women can drink no more than just one glass of alcohol a day (wine or beer), while men can drink two.

I know changing eating habits can be hard to do mostly because we found great pleasure in our food, but keep in mind that they're only habits. It's not so difficult to replace butter with olive oil and cook more with an oven or microwave than the frying pan. They're just habits.

Getting started in your kitchen

Start to open your kitchen cupboards and read the labels of what you eat. Look at sodium and fat content and decide if this food is good for your health or not. Basic changes to your daily nutrition habits can make a difference.

Considering to change the fat type you usually consume.

Here are some tips to let you decide what to start and what habit is important to change forever. As we said in the previous chapters, there are "good fats" and "bad fats", HDL, the first, and LDL, the second. When we eat we take both, but what we eat determines the quantity of them.

Eating butter, salami, sausages, hot dogs and fatty cheese is eating saturated fat.

Eating fried or packaged food, is eating trans-fat.

These are not good fats for our bodies. So their assumption might be limited to 5-6 % of the amount of daily calories for saturated fats and 1-2% for trans-fat. The safe quantity is so small that you can easily understand how bad is this food for you.

Avoid or reduce Salt and use spices and herbs.

Avoid salt or reduce it as much as possible. Instead of salt you can add lemon or lime juice or vinegar. You can also use spices like oregano, turmeric, garlic, basil, onion powder and coriander. Using spices adds to your food more than a simple flavor. Herbs provide potential benefits to your body.

- Ginger, pepper and chili have anti-inflammatory properties and may improve blood lipid levels.

- Cinnamon relaxes blood vessels, improves circulation and allows blood to flow, contributing to reducing blood pressure.

- Cayenne pepper reduces plaque buildup in arteries.

- Garlic can help prevent clogged arteries, helps arteries dilate and boosts circulation, and improves heart health by reducing blood pressure.

Reduce dairy products

Research about dairy has returned complex results. They contain saturated and ruminant trans fats, so can increase LDL cholesterol, but it depends on who is the person and what type of dairy product is consumed.

Dairy products are not all equal and while they're important to get enough calcium and vitamin D for women, at the same time, they're full of fats, that's not quite good for blood vessels.

Reducing their quantity is the best thing to do, but also choosing low-fat dairy, calcium and vitamins added, leaves us to use them in our recipes.

Low-fat (skimmed) milk, yogurt 0% fat and unflavoured yogurt, low-fat ricotta, low-fat cottage cheese and hard cheese are better options for people with heart disease or high cholesterol.

Avoid butter that can be replaced by olive oil, avocado, or nut butter. Avoid ice cream, cream and dairy desserts too. They're not part of a heart-healthy pattern.

Alternatives: soy milk, light cream cheese; almond, coconut, rice, or hemp milk; soy-based cheeses; low-fat cottage cheese; 0% fat greek yogurt.

Fresh seasonal fruits and vegetables.

Eat a lot of greens, raw or cooked vegetables are the best choice for your health. You can mix vegetables into your pasta, soups, and meat or fish recipes.

Starting your meal with a cup of raw vegetables helps you to lose weight more quickly and adds vitamins and minerals to your body.

Vegetables best choice: cucumbers, broccoli, kale, escarole, zucchini, yellow and red peppers, cauliflower, tomatoes, eggplant, and yellow squash.

Fresh fruits: avocado, oranges, pears, banana, apple, papaya, figs, mandarins, grapefruit, berries, pineapple, mangoes, grapes, plantains, apricot, watermelon.

Fresh fruit doesn't need any sugar added and can be used to make a simple dessert with a cup of reduced-fat yogurt or light ricotta cheese.

Whether vegetables and fruits are fresh or canned they are full of vitamins, minerals, potassium, magnesium and fiber. But don't forget to buy no-sugar and no-salt-added products when canned.

Oils and fats alternatives

- *Almond, walnut, nuts, sunflowers, peanuts or sesame seeds;*
- *Olive, peanuts, sesame and walnut cooking oils;*
- *Non-fat cooking sprays.*

Olive oil, a monounsaturated fat, is part of the "healthy" fat group of the mediterranean diet. The health benefits attributed to olive oil are specifically related to its high nutritional quality and positive effects on health.

About Proteins.

Even if meat is an important source of protein for us, bacon, pork and hamburger have a high content of saturated-fat. That is the reason why the American Heart Association suggests to consume fish, poultry without skin and other protein sources.

Changing our meat eating habits is not really easy, but limiting meat recipes 3-4 times a week and halving portions could be a good starting point. Do not forget legumes like lentils, dried peas and beans. Their high protein content makes them great substitutes to meat.

Be careful with canned legumes, they're excellent, but be aware at sodium content reading labels. In case they have sodium drain and rinse them well before use. There are lots of types for lentils and beans, use them all. They work well with soups or salads.

Try to eat fish at least twice a week, salmon, trout and sardine are good choices. Fish is a good source of Omega-3 fatty acids that ensures circulatory efficiency and promotes your heart health.

Whole grains and cereals.

They're the major source of energy and fiber for us. Rice, oats, corn and other cereals are all grains. There are two types of grains, whole and refined. Whole grain is the better choise for health, because they store nutrients and fibers our body needs.

Eat cereals with no added sugar for breakfast, like oatmeal, and brown rice, quinoa, whole oats, buckwheat at lunch or dinner. Whole grain muffins, bread and bagels are always good, and if you don't find them ready, you can cook them by yourself.

Legumes, seeds and nuts.

As we said before, legumes are a great source of protein, but also of minerals, potassium and magnesium. You can include some small portions in your daily meals, since they're high in calories, add seeds and nuts to your salads, or just as a snack.

Lentils, beans and dried peas can be boiled and combined with vegetables to have great mediterranean style salads.

Drink water.

Steer clear of sodas, smoothies, coke and fruit juices.

You can have your lunch or dinner with water and, if you like it, with a slice of lemon or orange inside.

There is a lot of sugar in drinks and sometimes also caffeine, that's not good for your heart health. If you like orange juice at breakfast you can make it by yourself with fresh fruits and no sugar inside.

How to store food.

As we use fresh ingredients in our recipes, how we store them is really important.

Check the stars of your freezer to know how many days your food can be stored and buy the exact quantity you need.

It's a good idea to cook more and store food in sized portions, well packed and labeled with the date, so you have packed lunches ready for working days.

The importance of total amount of calories

Eating food with low fat and low sodium doesn't mean you can eat without counting calories. Calories should not be more than the amount you expend with physical activity and through body metabolism.

Remember that menopause has changed your metabolism and you need a smaller amount than before. So check it with your doctor to find out what intakes are best for you.

High Sodium Content Food

- Smoked, cured, salted or canned meat, fish or poultry including bacon, cold cuts, ham, frankfurters, sausages, sardines, caviar and anchovies.
- Frozen breaded meats and dinners, such as burritos and pizza
- Canned entrees, such as ravioli, spam and chili
- Beans canned with salt added
- Ham, cheese, vegetable juice, salad dressing.

High Cholesterol Content Food

- Full-fat dairy foods such as milk, cheese, yogurt and cream.
- Animal fats, such as butter, ghee, margarine and spreads made from animal fats, lard, suet, and dripping.
- Fatty meat and processed meat products such as sausages.
- Lean meat such as liver, kidney, sweetbreads, heart and tripe
- Prawns, crab, lobster, squid, octopus and cuttlefish.
- Eggs

How to Make Heart Healthy Meals

Cooking food for a heart healthy diet plan doesn't mean you have to give up on taste. Here are some tips on how to have a good taste in a healthy recipe.

Cooking methods

- *Use non-sticking pans*
- *You can grill, roast, bake, microwave, steam, boil, lightly stir fry with cooking spray or a teaspoon of vegetable oil.*
- *Stew meat, chicken or turkey for a long time, left them cool and take out fat.*
- *Slow cooker lets your food have much more nutrients.*

Oil and butter

Avoid all fats hard at room temperature and replace them with a small amount of vegetable oil.

Spray oil is better than normal oil, we can use less.

Soft margarine is not really good to bake. In cakes, you can use a small amount of extra virgin olive oil and low-fat ricotta cheese or 0% fat greek yogurt. If you don't like the extra virgin olive oil taste, use other seed oil.

Use margarine low in saturated and trans fat, generally, they are made with vegetable oil.

Milk and Cream

Use skimmed milk instead of whole milk and unsalted low-fat cottage cheese or light ricotta or 0% fat greek yogurt instead of cream and sour cream.

0% fat greek yogurt is a good choice for cakes and biscuits, you can add a teaspoon of vegetable oil to have grease cake needs.

Use low-fat ricotta cheese in the same way as greek yogurt for your cookies.

How to replace eggs in cakes

In baking and cooking replacing 1 egg with 1/2 mature banana makes the dough moist and soft. Remember to add less sugar.

Replacing with 0% fat yogurt also gives dough softness. This is the best solution for muffins.

Replacing with cornstarch or potato starch needs to add some water. Remember to consider their nutrient facts in your food.

You can also use 3 egg whites and 1 egg yolk instead of 2 whole eggs.

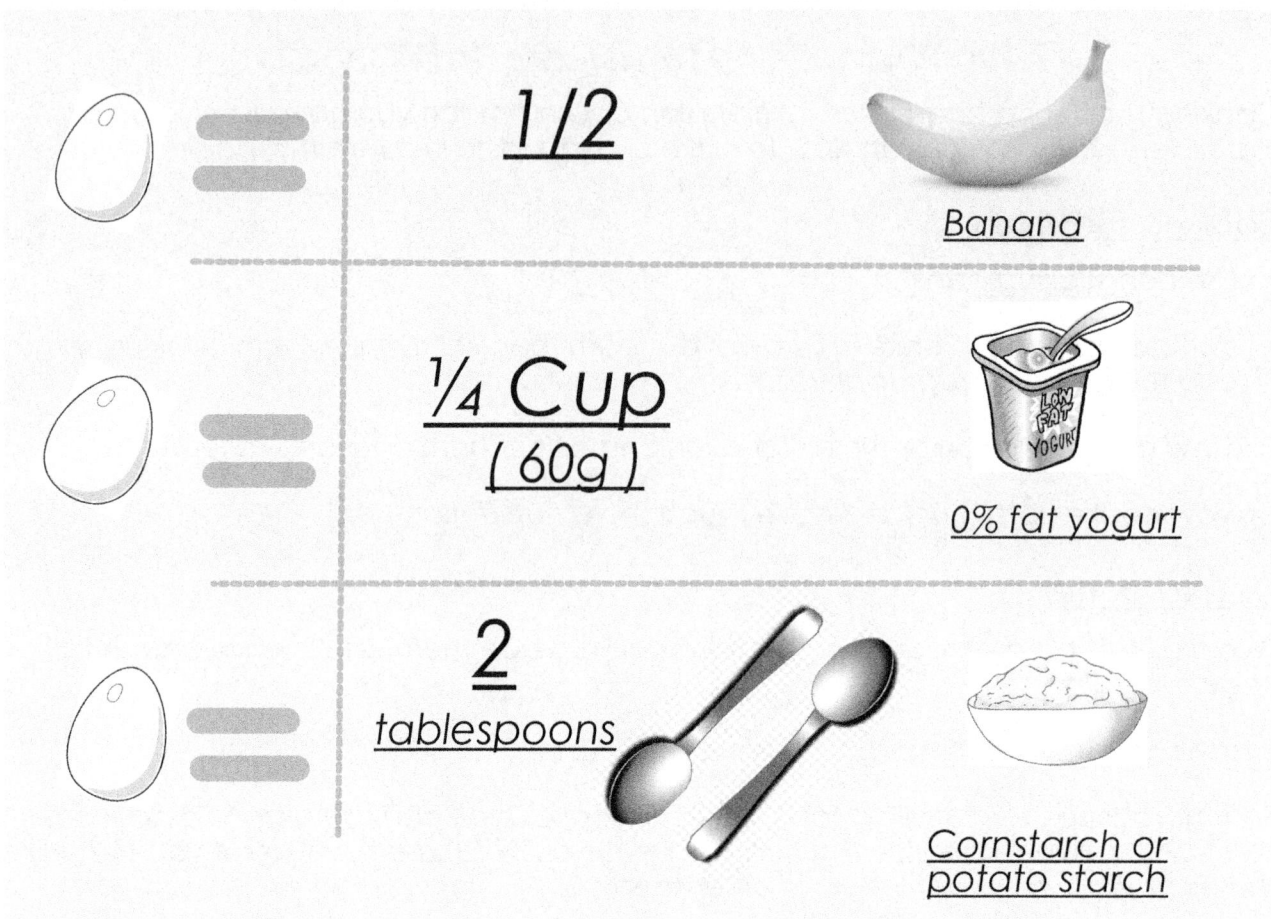

Tips and tricks

Use spices and herbs instead of salt. Remove skin from poultry and fat from meat. Substitute turkey for beef and pork meat. Remember to change your habits. Try to eat half portions, because a calorie is a calorie, whatever its source.

Kitchen Conversion Tables

Dry Measurements (approximate)

Cups	Grams	Ounces	Pounds	Tbspoons	Tspoons
1 cup	128 g	4.5 oz	0.28 lbs	16 tbsp	48 tsp
3/4 cup	96 g	3.38 oz	0.21 lbs	12 tbsp	36 tsp
2/3 cup	85 g	3 oz	0.19 lbs	10 tbsp	32 tsp
1/2 cup	64 g	2.25 oz	0.14 lbs	8 tbsp	24 tsp
1/3 cup	43 g	1.5 oz	0.09 lbs	5 tbsp	16 tsp
1/4 cup	32 g	1.13 oz	0.07 lbs	4 tbsp	12 tsp
1/8 cup	16 g	0.5 oz	0.03 lbs	2 tbsp	6 tsp

Liquid Measurements (approximate)

Cups	Tablespoons	Teaspoons	Milliliters
		1 tsp	5 ml
1/6 cup	1 tbsp	3 tsp	15 ml
1/8 cup	2 tbsp	6 tsp	30 ml
1/4 cup	4 tbsp	12 tsp	60 ml
1/3 cup	5 1/3 tbsp	16 tsp	80 ml
1/2 cup	8 tbsp	24 tsp	120 ml
2/3 cup	10 2/3 tbsp	32 tsp	160 ml
3/4 cup	12 tbsp	36 tsp	180 ml
1 cup	16 tbsp	48 tsp	237 ml
2 cups	32 tbsp		473 ml
4 cups	1 quart		946 ml
1 pint	32 tbsp		473 ml
2 pints	1 quart		946 ml (0.946 liters)
8 pints	4 quarts		3.785 ml (3.78 liters)
4 quarts	1 gallon		3.785 ml (3.78 liters)

Oven Temperature

Fahrenheit	Celsius
225° F	107° C
250° F	121° C
275° F	135° C
300° F	149° C
325° F	162° C
350° F	176° C
375° F	190° C
400° F	204° C
425° F	218° C
450° F	232° C
475° F	246° C
500° F	260° C

5 Weeks Meal Plans

Understanding your meals

These meal plans are:

low- sodium (1.500 milligrams per day is the recommended amount to low your blood pressure)

low-fat (cholesterol 200mg per day is the maximum recommended amount to low your cholesterol)

1500 calories a day (daily meals are planned for less than 1500 calories, so you can add milk or drinks. Remember you can have just 1 glass of wine or beer per day. Add calories to your daily amount.

The total amount of calories and nutrients you need is based on your style of life. They're based on age, body size, and level of activity. Ask your dietitian or doctor to know your calorie needs.

There is no salt at all in recipes. The amount of sodium comes from food.

If you want to add salt, look at the amount of sodium below.

Approximate amount of sodium in 1 teaspoon

Iodized table salt, fine = 2,300 mg	Kosher salt, course = 1,920 mg
Sea salt, fine = 2,120 mg	Sea salt, course = 1,560 mg
Pink Himalayan salt = 2,200 mg	Black salt = 1,150 - 2,200 mg

	Breakfast	Lunch	Dinner	Meal Plan week 1
Mon	Apple Pie Bread	Orecchiette Pasta with Broccoli Florets	Creamy Mushrooms Soup + Mediterranean Grilled Chicken	Calories 1253 Cholest 154 mg Sodium 404 mg Sat Fat 1 0,8 g
Tue	Orange low-fat Yogurt Muffins (2 Muffins)	Fresh Zucchini Pie + Low Fat Chicken Empanadas	Sweet Potato and Kale Salad + Blackened Cod & Tomato Basil Salad	Calories 1301 Cholest 132,5 mg Sodium 385,5 mg Sat Fat 8 g
Wed	Breakfast Burrito Recipe + Whole Wheat Tortilla	1/2 Lemon Pepper Roasted Chickpeas + Easy Grilled Pineapple Chicken	Stuffed Pepper Soup	Calories 1371 Cholest 100mg Sodium 529mg Sat.Fat 14,8g
Thu	Strawberries Almond Chia Pudding	Spinach & Ricotta Spaghetti	Crispy Lemon Sea Bass + Low Fat Strawberry Shortcake	Calories 1252 Cholest 16.8mg Sodium 461.8mg Sat Fat 8.1g
Fri	Cherry and Pistachios Yogurt Parfait	Fresh Zucchini Pie + Oatmeal Almond and Bluenerries Granola Bar	Baked Turkey Meatballs + Glazed Carrot and Sweet Potato Salad	Calories 1393 Cholest 116,3mg Sodium 515.5mg Sat Fat 7.4 g
Sat	Apple Pie Bread	Harvest Pumpkin Soup	Easy Grilled Pineapple Chicken + Tuscny Panzanella Salad	Calories 1282 Cholest 146mg Sodium 506.8mg Sat Fat 9,5 g
Sun	Orange Low Fat Yogurt Muffin (3 Muffins)	Catfish and Cherry Tomatoes	Easy Mexican Taco Turkey Meatloaf + Southwestern Bean Salad	Calories 1264 Cholest 147,6mg Sodium 532,8mg SatFat 8,6 g

	Breakfast	Lunch	Dinner	Meal Plan week 2
Mon	Vanilla Yogurt with Walnut and Apple + Lemon and Ricotta Italian Frittelle	Chicken and Black Kale Pasta Skillet	Chunky Vegetables Lentils Soup + Dark Chocolate Pistachio Fudge Balls (3 balls)	Calories 1414 Cholest 11,3 mg Sodium 662,1mg Sat Fat 9,6 g
Tue	Toast with Ricotta Cheese and Sun-Dried Tomatoes	Lemon Chickpeas Quinoa Salad	Grilled Tandoori Catfish + Blackberries Rice Pudding	Calories 1207 Cholest 9.9 mg Sodium 482.6mg Sat Fat 2,7 g
Wed	Starbucks Pumpkin Scone Copycat recipe	Orecchiette Pasta with Broccoli Florets	Turkey Long Grain Rice Soup + Dairy-Free Iced Mocha Latte	Calories 1261 Cholest 154,2mg Sodium 737.4mg Sat.Fat 5,5 g
Thu	Easy Butter-Free British Dried Fruit Flapjack	Lentils and Celery Ditalini Pasta + Super Easy Vanilla Banana Mug Cake	Curried Mushrooms and Cauliflower Soup + Salmon Salad with Orange Vinaigrette	Calories 1235 Cholest 22.5mg Sodium 207.7mg Sat Fat 11,8 g
Fri	Low Fat Chicken Empanadas	Cruncy Veggie Chips + Baked Turkey Meatballs	Red Bell Pepper Macaroni + Almond Vanilla Fruit Salad + Dark Chocolate Pistachio Fudge Balls (1 ball)	Calories 1154 Cholest 129.1mg Sodium 277.1mg Sat Fat 11,4 g
Sat	Healthy Banana Nut Pancakes	Southern Bean Salad + Orange Chicken Cutlet	Broccoli Cheese Soup	Calories 1341 Cholest 142.5mg Sodium 749mg Sat Fat 4,9 g
Sun	Rice Pudding with Blueberries and Figs	1 Ricotta Bread Roll + Edamame Guacamole + Mediterranean Grilled Chicken	Artichokes and Black olives Fettuccine + Healthy Pistachio and Date Raw Bites (2)	Calories 1308 Cholest 77 mg Sodium 459.8mg SatFat 8.6g g

	Breakfast	Lunch	Dinner	<ins>Meal Plan week 3</ins>
Mon	Banana Oats Muffin (1)	Easy Honey Garlic Salmon + Tomato Cucumber Salad	Baked Zucchini and Potatoes Sticks + Easy Baked Boneless Chicken Thighs	Calories 1204 Cholest 80 mg Sodium 289 mg Sat Fat 6 g
Tue	Avocado Banana Smoothie + 1 Light Oats Wholemeal Cookie	Bamboo Piadina (1) + Eggplant and Tomatoes Skillet + Italian Marinara Meatballs (2)	Red Bell Pepper Macaroni	Calories 1136 Cholest 50.8 mg Sodium 324.3 mg Sat Fat 12.1 g
Wed	Vanilla Yogurt with Peach and Pear + Homemade Super Easy Oatmeal Cookies (2)	Sheet Pan Teriyaki Salmon + Beetroot Cutlet (2)	Tomato and Basil Caprese Pasta Salad	Calories 1439 Cholest 142,8mg Sodium 758,2mg Sat.Fat 8.3g
Thu	Strawberries Almond Chia Pudding	Spanakopita Greek Savory Pie	Homemade Ground Turkey Burgers (1) + Red and Yellow Bell Pepper with Zucchini	Calories 1288 Cholest 133.4mg Sodium 624.9mg Sat Fat 4.8g
Fri	Pumpkin Banana Bread Baked Oatmeal	Eggplant and Ricotta Rigatoni	Tomato Cucumber Salad + Beef and Barley Soup	Calories 1119 Cholest 141.3mg Sodium 581.8mg Sat Fat 8.7g
Sat	Homemade Super Easy Oatmeal Cookies (3)	Healthy Shrimps Spaghetti Italian-Style	Sweet Potato and Kale Salad + Orange and Onion Chicken	Calories 1218 Cholest 69mg Sodium 55.9mg Sat Fat 5.8g
Sun	Low Fat Chicken Empanadas	Tuscany Panzanella Salad + Low Fat Hazelnut and Pear Flan	Flounder Fillets and Black Olive Tomato Soup + Bamboo Piadina (1) + Veggie Potato Gateau	Calories 1137 Cholest 235mg Sodium 510.9mg SatFat 7.4g

	Breakfast	Lunch	Dinner	Meal Plan week 4
Mon	French Toast with Strawberries	Tuscany Ribollita Italian Recipe	Grilled Tandoori Catfish + Coconut Banana Ice Cream	Calories 1145 Cholest 2.5mg Sodium 764.4mg Sat Fat 6.5g
Tue	Strawberry Almon Chia Pudding	Dairy-Free Chicken Pot Pie	Walnut and Basil Penne Pasta + Chocolate Dip Frozen Bananas	Calories 1344 Cholest 0mg Sodium 502.8mg Sat Fat 10.4g
Wed	Apple Pie Bread	Harvest Pumpkin Soup	Easy Grilled Pineapple Chicken + Tuscany Panzanella Salad	Calories 1282 Cholest 146mg Sodium 506.8mg Sat Fat 9,5 g
Thu	Toast with Ricotta Cheese and Sun-Dried Tomatoes	Lemon Chickpea Quinoa Salad	Grilled Tandoori Catfish + Blackberries Rice Pudding	Calories 1207 Cholest 9.9 mg Sodium 482.6mg Sat Fat 2,7 g
Fri	Breakfast Burrito Recipe + Whole Wheat Tortilla	1/2 Lemon Pepper Roasted Chickpeas + Easy Grilled Pineapple Chicken	Stuffed Pepper Soup	Calories 1371 Cholest 100mg Sodium 529mg Sat.Fat 14,8g
Sat	Vanilla Yogurt with Walnut and Apple + Lemon and Ricotta Italian Frittelle	Chicken and Black Kale Pasta Skillet	Chunky Vegetables Lentils Soup + Dark Chocolate Pistachio Fudge Balls (3 balls)	Calories 1414 Cholest 11,3 mg Sodium 662,1mg Sat Fat 9,6 g
Sun	Banana Oats Muffin (1)	Easy Honey Garlic Salmon + Tomato Cucumber Salad	Baked Zucchini and Potatoes Sticks + Easy Baked Boneless Chicken Thighs	Calories 1204 Cholest 80 mg Sodium 289 mg Sat Fat 6 g

	Breakfast	Lunch	Dinner	Meal Plan week 5
Mon	Chocolate and Orange Muffins (2 Muffins)	Creamy Mushroom Soup + Low Fat Chicken Empanadas	Lemon Baked Cod + Fresh Zucchini Pie	Calories 1204 Cholest 151.4mg Sodium 451.3mg Sat Fat 10g
Tue	Starbucks Pumpkin Scone Copycat recipe	Orecchiette Pasta with Broccoli Florets	Turkey Long Grain Rice Soup + Dairy-Free Iced Mocha Latte	Calories 1261 Cholest 154,2mg Sodium 737.4mg Sat.Fat 5,5 g
Wed	Lighy Oats Wholemeal Cookies (3)	Lemon Chickpea Quinoa Salad	Parsley Lime Halibut Fillets + Baked Zucchini and Potato Sticks + Healthy Pistachio and Date Raw Bites (2)	Calories 1207 Cholest 0mg Sodium 393.4mg Sat Fat 1 5.6 g
Thu	Rice Pudding with Blueberries and Figs	1 Ricotta Bread Roll + Edamame Guacamole + Mediterranean Grilled Chicken	Artichokes and Black olives Fettuccine + Healthy Pistachio and Date Raw Bites (2)	Calories 1308 Cholest 77 mg Sodium 459.8mg SatFat 8.6g g
Fri	Pumpkin Banana Bread Baked Oatmeal	Eggplant and Tomato Skillet Italian-Style + Grilled Snapper in Orange Sauce	Fresh Zucchini Pie + Blackberries Rice Pudding	Calories 1353 Cholest 146.9mg Sodium 605.3mg Sat Fat 5.6g
Sat	Chocolate and Orange Muffins (1)	Summer Greens with Apple and Almond +Italian Marinara Meatballs (3)	Catfish and Cherry Tomatoes Pasta	Calories 1230 Cholest 114.7mg Sodium 300.9mg Sat Fat 8,7g
Sun	Lemon and Ricotta Italian Frittelle	One-Pot Meat Sauce Pasta Recipe	Pepper Crusted Ahi Tuna and Aragula Salad + Low Fat Yummy Strawberry Shortcake	Calories 1336 Cholest 127mg Sodium 363.1mg SatFat 10.5g

Low-Sodium Low-Fat Snacks

Celery Sticks with Cream Cheese Mousse

10 min. / 2 servings / Easy

Ingredients

- 2 rinsed celery sticks
- 1/8 cup (16 g) low-fat cream cheese
- 1/8 cup (16 g) 0% fat greek yogurt
- 1/2 tbsp chopped walnuts
- 1 tsp lemon juice
- 1 tbsp chopped green onion
- Pepper to taste

Mix well, with a spoon, cream cheese, yogurt, lemon juice, onions and pepper. Cut each stick into 4 pieces and spread the mixture down in the middle. Garnish with chopped walnuts.

Serving: 1 Total fat: 2 g Saturated Fat: 1 g Calories: 35 Cholesterol: 4 mg Protein: 2 g Carbo: 3 g Fiber: 1 g Sodium: 58 mg

Oatmeal Almonds and Blueberries Granola Bar

30 min / 6 servings / Easy /Oven

Ingredients:

- 1/2 cup (70g) almonds
- 1/2 cup (60g) dried blueberries
- 1/2 cup (60g) dried grapes
- 1 cup (80g) rolled oats
- 1/8 cup (16g) flaxseed
- 1 tsp olive oil
- 1/4 cup (60ml) maple syrup

Preheat the oven to 350°F. Mix together all the ingredients until they're well combined and sticky. Spread the mix into a baking sheet and bake for about 10- 15 minutes. Cut into 6 slices.

Serving size:1 Total Fat: 9.4 g Saturated Fat: 2 g Trans Fat: 0 Calories: 278 Cholesterol: 0 Protein: 7.9 Potassium: 411 mg Carbo: 40 g Fiber: 8.7 g Sugar:13.6 g Sodium: 41 mg

Lemon Pepper Roasted Chickpeas

30 min. / 3 servings / Easy / Oven

Ingredients:

- 1 x 15 oz can of low-sodium chickpeas (400g)
- 2 tbsp extra virgin olive oil
- 1 tbsp fresh onion or garlic chopped (what you like more)
- 1 lemon, juice and zest
- 1 tsp basil
- 1 tsp oregano
- Pepper to taste

Preheat oven to 450° F. Roll chickpeas, well rinsed and drained, in a paper towel to remove skins. Put oil, chickpeas and spices in a bowl and mix well. Spread on a baking sheet and bake for 20 minutes. Let cool completely before eating.

Serving size: 1 Total Fat: 12 g Saturated Fat: 1.3 g Trans Fat: 0 Calories: 260 Cholesterol: 0 Protein: 7.9 g Potassium: 32 mg Carbo: 28 g Fiber: 8 g Sugar: 5.4 g Sodium: 222 mg

Tzatziki Dip

30 min. / 3 Servings / Easy /

Ingredients:

- 1/2 cup (120g) 0% fat greek yogurt
- 1 garlic clove, minced
- 2 tbsp lemon juice
- 1/4 cup (120g) shredded cucumber
- 2 tbsp of fresh chopped dill
- Pepper to taste
- 3-4 slices of lemon and cucumber to garnish

Shred cucumber and place it into a towel to squeeze out any excess liquid. Add in a bowl garlic, lemon, cucumber, and fresh dill and mix well. Add yogurt and stir all together. Season with pepper as taste. Let it sit in the fridge for 3-4 hours.

Serving size: 1 Total Fat: 9.4 g Saturated Fat: 2 g Trans Fat: 0 Calories: 297 Cholesterol: 0 Protein: 7.9g Potassium: 131 mg Carbo: 45 g Fiber: 9.4 g Sugar: 22.9 g Sodium: 58 mg

Peanut Butter Hummus

20 min. / 6 servings / Easy / Fodd processor

Ingredients:

- 1 x 15 oz can of low-sodium chickpeas (400g)
- 1 garlic clove, minced
- 2 tbsp lemon juice
- 2 tbsp Peanut Butter
- 1 tsp extra virgin olive oil
- 1/2 tsp paprika
- 3-4 tbsp of water

Put all the ingredients in a food processor and mix them. Season with pepper if you like. Place in a bowl and serve with whole grain pitas or celery sticks.

Serving size: 1 Total Fat: 5 g Saturated Fat: 0.8 g Trans Fat: 0 Calories: 130 Cholesterol: 0 Protein: 5.6 g Potassium: 18.9 mg Carbo: 15 g Fiber: 4.4 g Sugar: 2.9 g Sodium: 123 mg

Crunchy Veggie Chips

3 hours / 3 servings / Easy / Oven

Ingredients

- 1 cup sweet potato (140g)
- 1 cup beets (140g)
- 1 tbsp extra virgin olive oil

Preheat oven to 200° F. Use a mandoline to slice beets and potatoes extra-thin for the optimum crunch. Grease with olive oil slices and spread onto a paper sheet. Bake for about 3 hours or until crunch.

Serving size: 1 Total Fat: 1.6 g Saturated Fat: 0.3 g Trans Fat: 0 Calories: 77 Cholesterol: 0 Protein: 1.7 g Potassium: 369 mg Carbo: 14 g Fiber: 3 g Sugar: 6 g Sodium: 0

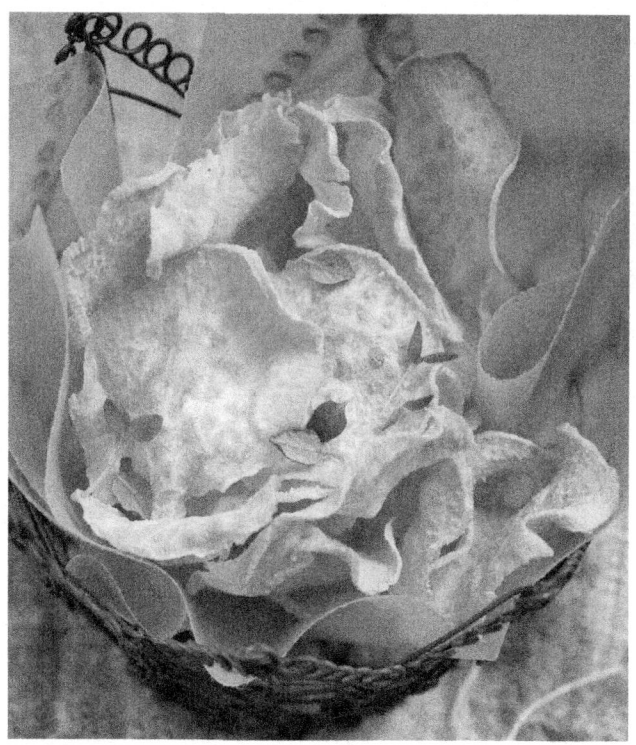

Vanilla Yogurt with Peach and Pear

2 Hours / 3 Servings / Easy / Food Processor

Ingredients:

- 1cup (240g) 0% fat greek yogurt

- 1 banana (140g)
- 3-4 tbsp of cold water
- 2 tbsp lemon juice
- 1/2 cup (85g) diced frozen peach
- 1/2 cup (85g) diced frozen pear
- 2-3 drops of vanilla extract.
- 1 tsp stevia sweetener
- 6 walnut to garnish

Blend frozen peach and pear in a food processor with water, stevia and lemon juice until smooth. Cover and re-freeze for 20-30 minutes. Whisk banana with yogurt and vanilla in the food processor, cover and freeze for at least 1 hour. Let the yogurt sit at room temperature for 10 to 15 minutes before serving. Divide vanilla yogurt into 3 small bowls and add the frozen fruits on top. Garnish with 2 walnuts each.

Serving size: 1 Total Fat: 3.3 g Saturated Fat: 0 Trans Fat: 0 Calories: 170 Cholesterol: 0 Protein: 9.3 g Potassium: 254 mg Carbo: 23 g Fiber: 2.4 g Sugar: 19.4 g Sodium: 49 mg

Vanilla Yogurt with Walnut and Apple

10 min / 3 servings / Easy

Ingredients:

- 1 cup (240g) 0% fat greek yogurt
- 1 banana (140g)
- 2 tbsp of cold water
- 1 tbsp lemon juice
- 1 cup (170g) diced apple
- 2-3 drops of vanilla extract.
- 1 tsp stevia sweetener
- 12 chopped walnut

Blend frozen apples in a food processor with water, stevia and lemon juice until smooth. Cover and re-freeze for 20-30 minutes. Whisk banana with yogurt and vanilla in the food processor, cover and freeze for at least 1 hour. Let the yogurt sit at room temperature for 10 to 15 minutes. Divide vanilla yogurt into 3 small bowls and add the frozen fruits and chopped walnut on top.

Serving size: 1 Total Fat: 6 g Saturated Fat: 0 Trans Fat: 0 Calories: 180 Cholesterol: 0 Protein: 9.3 g Potassium: 259 mg Carbo: 22 g Fiber: 2.1 g Sugar: 14.7 g Sodium: 68 mg

Low-Fat Chicken Empanadas

1 hour / 10 servings / Medium / Oven

Ingredients:

- 1 pound (450g) chicken breast
- 2 garlic cloves, minced
- 1/2 cup (85g) carrot, sliced
- 1 cup (60g) fresh chopped spinach
- 2 tbsp chopped onion
- 1/2 tsp black pepper
- 3 champignon mushrooms
- 1/2 cup (90g) low-fat cream cheese
- 1 tbsp chili powder
- 2 tbsp extra virgin olive oil

For dough:
- 1 & 1/2 cups (195g) W. W. flour
- 2/3 cup (150gr) water

Cook slowly in a wok, with 2 tbsp of oil, the minced chicken breast with chopped spinach, carrots, mushrooms, onion and garlic for 10-15 minutes. Mix in a bowl the flour with the water and make an elastic dough.

Divide into 10 pieces and roll them out in a thin pita.

Fill them with 1 big tbsp of veggie meat, add 1 tsp of low-fat cheese and close half-moon-shaped.

Put empanadas on a paper sheet, lightly wet with oil and bake at 450 degrees F. for about 20 minutes.

Serving size: 1 Total Fat: 6 g Saturated Fat: 1.7 g Trans Fat: 0 Calories: 180 Cholesterol: 41 mg Protein: 17.5 g Potassium: 138 mg Carbo: 14 g Fiber: 2.9 g Sugar: 1.2 g Sodium: 55.3 mg

Lemon & Ricotta Italian Frittelle

15 min / 4 servings / Easy / Oven

Ingredients:

- 3/4 cup (165g) low fat ricotta cheese
- 2 tbsp olive oil
- 1 tbsp maple syrup
- 1 cup (130g) whole wheat flour
- 1 lemon, zest and juice
- 2 egg whites
- 1 tsp baking powder
- 1 tbsp powdered sugar to garnish

Preheat oven to 400° F.

Mix in a bowl egg whites and syrup, add ricotta, lemon juice and zest, oil and whisk well.

Add all the flour and baking powder e mix with a wooden spoon. With a spoon make 20 little balls on a paper sheet and bake for 10-12 minutes in the oven at 400 degrees F.

You can also bake frittelle with Air Fryer.

Garnish with powdered sugar.

Serving size: 1 Total Fat: 7.6 g Saturated Fat: 1 g Trans Fat: 0 Calories: 237 Cholesterol: 11.3 mg Protein: 10.4 g Potassium: 49 mg Carbo: 32 g Fiber: 4 g Sugar: 10.8 g Sodium: 206 mg

Choccolate-Dipped Frozen Banana

1 hour + 15 min / 6 servings / Easy

Ingredients

- 1 banana (100g)
- 4 oz (110g) unsweetened dark chocolate baking bar
- 1/3 cup (40g) shelled walnuts, chopped
- 6 wooden sticks

Cut banana into 6 pieces and skewer with a wooden stick, place on a paper sheet and freeze for 1 hour.

Place chopped chocolate in a microwave-safe bowl and melt it in 30-second increments until smooth and melted.

Cover banana pieces with melted chocolate, helping you with a spoon.

Cover with chopped walnuts and serve after 10 minutes or freeze them again.

Serving size: 1 Total Fat: 14 g Saturated Fat: 6.4 g Trans Fat: 0 Calories: 184 Cholesterol: 0.7 mg Protein: 3.8 g Potassium: 247.7 mg Carbo: 10 g Fiber: 4.2 g Sugar: 2.7 g Sodium: 4.8 mg

Edamame Guacamole

30 min / 10 servings / Easy / Food Processor

Ingredients

- 1 cup (240g) shelled edamame
- 3 medium avocados, chopped

- 1 Roma tomato chopped
- 2 tbsp of lime juice
- 2 tbsp of water
- 1/4 cup (15 g) chopped onion
- 1/2 medium fresh jalapeno, seeds and ribs discarded, chopped
- 1 garlic clove, finely chopped
- 1/4 cup (15 g) fresh cilantro
- 1/2 tsp cinnamon
- 3 tbsp extra virgin olive oil

Boil and drain edamame as indicated on the package.

Put it in the food processor bowl, but set aside 1 tbsp to garnish, add 2 tbsp of water and process until smooth.

Make sure all ingredients are finely chopped.

Mix up edamame puree with avocados, tomato, lime juice, onion, jalapeno, garlic, and cilantro. Stir with reserved edamame.

Divide guacamole into 10 serving sizes, using freezer bags.

Thaw at room temperature before serving. .

Serving size: 1 Total Fat: 10 g Saturated Fat: 1.4 g Trans Fat: 0 Calories: 116 Cholesterol: 0 Protein: 3.5 g Potassium: 349 mg Carbo: 3.1 g Fiber: 5.8 g Sugar: 1.5 g Sodium: 65.7 mg

Easy British Dried Fruit Flapjacks

30 Min / 10 servings / Easy / Oven

Ingredients

- 3 cups (240g) rolled oats
- 1/6 cup (20g) olive oil
- 1/6 cup (34g) brown sugar
- 2.5 tbsp maple syrup
- 1/6 cup (35g) mixed dried fruit

Preheat oven to 350° F.

IIn a small saucepan heat oil, sugar and syrup on low heat.

Stir continuously until the mixture resembles a caramel sauce. Mix oats and dried fruit in a bowl, pour the caramel in and stir until well combined.

Line an 8x8 inch baking pan with parchment paper, transfer the mixture and pack it down with the back of a spoon.

Bake for 20 minutes.

Allow to cool for 30 minutes before removing and cutting into squares.

Serving size: 1 Total Fat: 8.5 g Saturated Fat: 8.5 g Trans fat: 0 Calories: 237 Cholesterol: 0 Protein: 3.2 g Potassium. 143 mg Carbo: 37 Fiber: 3.1 g Sugar: 18.7 g Soduim: 6.5 mg

Low-Sodium Low-Fat Breakfast

Healthy Banana Nut Pancakes

15 min / 3 servings / Easy

Ingredients

- 1/2 cup (65g) whole wheat flour
- 1 medium ripe banana (126g)
- 1/2 cup (120ml) skimmed milk
- 1 tsp cinnamon
- 1 tbsp olive oil
- 1 tsp baking powder
- 2 egg whites
- 1 tsp vanilla extract
- 6 walnuts
- 3 tsp maple syrup

Combine all dry ingredients in a bowl. Beat egg whites until fluffy. Mix mashed banana with milk, oil and vanilla and add egg whites. Add wet ingredients to dry and mix, but do not overmix. Cook for 3-4 minutes on each side. You must have 6. Garnish 1 pancake with maple syrup and 2 walnuts.

Serving size: 1 Total Fat: 8.4 g Saturated Fat: 0.7 g Trans Fat 0 Calories: 229 Cholesterol. 0 Ptrotein: 7.5 g Potassium: 206 mg Carbo: 31 g Fiber: 4 g Sugar: 13.7 g Sodium: 237 mg

French Toast with Strawberries

15 min / 1 serving / Easy /

Ingredients

- 2 slices whole wheat bread (55g all)
- 1/2 cup (120ml) skimmed milk
- 2 egg whites
- 1 pinch cinnamon
- 1 pinch nutmeg
- 1/2 tbsp maple syrup
- 1/4 cup (60ml) fresh orange juice
- 1 tsp stevia sweetener
- 2-3 strawberries

Add all ingredients in a bowl, except bread and mix well. Dip bread slices on every side for 2-3 minutes or until they've absorbed all milk. Cook in a non-sticking pan with baking spray for 2 minutes on each side. Serve with strawberries or other fruits.

Serving size: 1 Total Fat: 2.2 g Satureted Fat: 0 Trans Fat: 0 Calories: 291 Cholesterol: 2.5 mg Protein: 7.4 g Potassium: 380 mg Carbo: 50 g Fiber: 3 g Sugar: 14 g Sodium: 471 mg

Apple-Pie Bread

1 hour / 12 serving / Medium / Oven

Ingredients

- 2 cups (260g) whole wheat flour
- 2/3 cup (150g) sugar
- 1/2 cup (120g) 0% fat greek yogurt
- 2/3 cup (130g) apple, mashed
- 1 tsp vanilla extract
- 1 egg
- 1 little ripe banana
- 5 tbsp olive oil
- 2 tbsp lemon juice + 2 of zest
- 2 tsp baking powder
- 1 tsp cinnamon
- 1/2 cup (65g) chopped walnuts
- 1 big apple diced
- 3 tbsp brown sugar

Preheat oven to 350° F. Mix in a bowl sugar, yogurt, ripe banana, 4 tbsp oil, lemon zest, lemon juice and egg until well combined. Add apple pureè, and vanilla, mix and set aside. Coat a 9-by-5-inch loaf pan with baking spray. Add in another bowl the flour (setting aside 1 tbsp) baking powder, and mix. Add chopped apple and stir until pieces are well coated. In a little dish combine walnuts, brown sugar, and cinnamon, with the remaining spoon of flour and spoon of oil and pour on the cake. Bake until a wooden pick inserted in the center of the loaf comes out clean, about 60 minutes.

Serving size: 1 Total Fat: 10 g Satureted Fat: 1 g Trans fat: 0 Calories: 245 Cholesterol: 16 mg Protein: 5.2 g Potassium: 58 mg Carbo: 33 g Fiber: 3.2 g Sugar: 18 g Sodium: 91 mg

Avocado Banana Smoothie

10 min / 2 servings / Easy / Food processor

Ingredients

- 1 1/2 cups (375g) unsweetened coconut milk
- 1 ripe avocado
- 1 ripe banana
- 1 cup (30g) chopped spinach
- 1 pinch ground cinnamon (top)

Place all the ingredients in a food processor and blend until you have a very fine smoothie. Serve cold with cinnamon on top.

Serving size: 1 Total Fat: 17.7 g Saturated Fat: 5 g Trans Fat: 0 Calories: 241 Cholesterol: 0 Protein: 3.7 g Potassium: 998.5 mg Carbo: 16.8 g Fiber: 8.5 g Sugar: 8.3 g Sodium: 96.3 mg

Banana Oats Muffins

40 min / 12 servings / Easy / Oven

Topping:

- 2 tbsp olive oil,
- 2 tbsp brown sugar,
- 1 pinch cinnamon,
- 1/2 cup (40g) rolled oats

Ingredients

- 1 & 1/2 cups (120g) old fashioned rolled oats
- 1 & 1/4 (160g) whole wheat flour
- 2 tsp baking powder
- 1/2 cup sugar
- 1 tsp cinnamon
- 2 egg whites
- 1/4 cup (33g) olive oil
- 1 & 1/2 cups (200g) mashed banana (about 3)

Preheat oven to 375° F. Mix all dry ingredients in a bowl. Mix all wet ingredients in another bowl, then whisk together. Pour into a 12-cup non-sticking muffin pan. Combine topping ingredients and sprinkle over the muffin. Bake for 20 minutes.

Serving size: 1 Total Fat: 5.7 g Saturated Fat: 0.7 g Trans Fat: 0 Calories: 199 Cholesterol: 0 mg Protein: 4.1 g Potassium: 132 mg Carbo: 32 g Fiber: 3.7 g Sugar: 13 g Sodium: 90.7 mg

Chocolate and Orange Muffins

30 min / 12 servings / Easy / Oven

Ingredients:

- 2 & 1/2 cups (300g) whole wheat flour
- 1/2 cup (80g) chocolate drops
- 2 tbsp baking powder
- 3 tbsp olive oil
- 1/3 cup (80ml) skimmed milk
- 1/3 cup (80ml) orange juice
- 1 orange zest
- 1/2 cup (100g) granulated sugar
- 1 egg + 2 egg whites

Preheat oven to 350° F. Whisk all ingredients together, without chocolate drops until you have a well-mixed dough. Add chocolate drops and pour into a 12-cup non-sticking muffin pan. Bake for about 20 minutes.

Serving size: 1 Totala Fat: 7.3 g Saturated Fat: 2.4 g Trans Fat: 0 Calories: 210 Cholesterol: 31 mg Protein: 4.9 g Potassium: 22 mg Carbo: 28 g Fiber: 2.8 g Sugar: 14 g Sodium: 96 mg

Rice Pudding with Blueberries and Figs

1 hour / 4 servings / Easy

Ingredients:

- 1/2 (cup 100g) short-grain brown rice
- 2 tbsp maple syrup
- 4 cups (1 Lt) unsweetened almond milk
- 1 tsp vanilla extract
- 1/2 tsp cinnamon
- 2 medium figs (100g)
- 1/2 cup (74g) fresh blueberries

Boil rice into the milk slowly until all liquid has been absorbed and reached pudding consistency. Add vanilla, cinnamon and mix well. Divide into 4 cups and garnish with maple syrup and fruit.

Serving size: 1 Total Fat: 3.4 g Satureted Fat: 0 Trans fat: 0 Calories: 165 Cholesterol: 16 mg Protein: 3.3 g Potassium: 252 mg Carbo: 28 g Fiber: 2.5 g Sugar: 112 g Sodium: 171 mg

Orange Low-Fat Yogurt Muffin

40 min / 18 muffins / Medium / Oven

Ingredients

- 1 & 1/4 cups (160g) whole wheat flour
- 1 egg + 2 egg whites
- 1/4 cup (60gr) skimmed milk
- 1/4 (50g) granulated sugar
- 1.6 oz (45g) 0% fat greek yogurt
- 3 tbsp olive oil
- 1 big orange zest and juice
- 1 tsp vanilla extract
- 2 tsp baking powder

Preheat the oven to 350° F.

In a bowl mix together all wet ingredients. In another bowl mix together all dry ingredients. Add wet ingredients into the dry ones and mix until moistened. Scoop into the prepared muffin pan 3/4 of the way. Bake for about 10 to 12 minutes.

Serving size: 1 Total Fat: 1.2 g Saturated Fat: 0.3 g Trans Fat: 0 Calories: 73 Cholesterol: 11.7 mg Protein: 4.9 g Potassium: 36.3 mg Carbo: 10.6 g Fiber: 1.1 g Sugar: 4.8 g Sodium: 80 mg

Cranberry Bliss Bars

40 min / 12 servings / Medium / Oven

Bar:
- 3 tbsp olive oil
- 1/4 cup (50g) brown sugar
- 1 cup (130g) whole wheat flour
- 2 tsp baking powder
- 1 tsp vanilla extract
- 1 tsp orange extract
- 1 egg + 2 egg whites
- 1/2 cup (85g) white chocolate chips
- 1/2 tsp ground ginger
- 1/2 cup (70g) craisins

Topping
- 1 cup (225g) low-fat cream cheese
- 1/2 tsp orange extract
- 1/2 vanilla extract
- 1/4 cup (30g) powdered sugar
- 1/4 cup (35g) chopped craisins
- 1 oz (30g) white baking chocolate

Preheat oven to 350° F.

Beat together oil, brown sugar, eggs, orange, and vanilla until well mixed. Add baking, ground ginger, white chocolate chips and craisins. Spread into the bottom of a prepared 15x10 pan.

Bake for 18-22 minutes until set and golden brown at the edges. Don't overbake or bars will be hard.

Topping: beat cream cheese, orange, vanilla and powdered sugar together with a food processor until smooth and creamy. Top cooled with frosting. Sprinkle with craisins and white chocolate on top.

Serving size: 1 Total Fat: 11.5 g Saturated Fat: 5.1 g Trans Fat: 0 Calories: 253 Cholesterol: 26.3 mg Protein: 4.8 g Potassium: 65 mg Carbo: 32.5 g Fiber: 2.1 g Sugar: 24.9 g Sodium: 111 mg

Cherry and Pistachio Yogurt Parfait

10 min / 2 servings / Easy

Ingredients:

- 1/4 cup (33g) unsalted shelled pistachios
- 1 cup (240g) 0% fat greek yogurt
- 1/2 cup (80g) dried tart cherries
- 1 tbsp maple syrup

Mix yogurt with maple syrup. Make layers of fruit, yogurt and pistachios in a glass. Refrigerate until ready to serve.

Serving size: 1 Total Fat: 13 g Saturated fat: 0 Trans fat: 0 Calories: 378 Cholesterol: 5 mg Protein: 19 g Potassium: 300 mg Carbo: 45 g Fiber: 4.5 g Sugar: 29 g Sodium: 178 mg

Apple Crisp Recipe

60 min / 4 servings / Easy / Oven

Ingredients:

- Filling: 2.5 cups (250g) sliced apples, 1/2 cup (100g) sugar, 1/2 tsp cinnamon, 1 tsp vanilla extract.
- Topping: 1/4 cup (160g) whole wheat flour, 1/2 cup (100g) brown sugar, 1/4 cup (20g) old fashioned rolled oats, 1/2 tsp cinnamon, 1 tbsp olive oil

Preheat oven to 350° F.

Combine all together the filling ingredients and pour into a greased pie dish. Combine all together the topping ingredients and sprinkle the crumb mixture over the top of the apples. Bake for 50 minutes.

Serving size: 1 Total Fat: 4 g Saturated Fat: 0.5 g Trans Fat: 0 Calorie: 319 Cholesterol: 0 Protein: 1.8 g Potassium: 83 mg Carbo: 69 g Fiber: 3.9 g Sugar: 57 g Sodium: 0

Strawberry Almond Chia Pudding

15 min + 4 hours / 2 servings / Easy

Strawberries chia mix: 6 oz (180g) strawberries, 1 tsp maple syrup, 1 tsp lemon juice, 1 tbsp chia seeds.

Cook strawberries in a pan with a tbsp or two of water for 6-7 minutes. Mash them with a fork. Add syrup, lemon and chia seeds, and let it stand for 5-10 minutes. Put into fridge.

Chia Pudding: 4 oz (120g) 0% fat greek yogurt, 1 & 1/2 cups (360ml) skimmed milk, 1 tsp maple syrup, 2 tbsp chia seeds, 1 tsp vanilla extract, 4-5 chopped almonds to garnish

Whisk together yogurt, milk, syrup, vanilla and chia seeds and put into the fridge for 4 hours or all night.

Later divide into 2 glasses, making layers of the 2 chia seeds mix. Garnish with chopped almonds

Serving size: 1 Total Fat: 5.9 g Saturated Fat: 0 Trans Fat: 0 Calories: 241 Cholesterol: 0 Protein: 17.9 g Potassium: 286 mg Carbo: 29 g Fiber: 9.5 g Sugar: 20 g Sodium: 140 mg

Toast with Ricotta Cheese and Sun-Dried Tomatoes

15 min / 1 serving / Easy

Ingredients
- 1 slice whole wheat bread (50g)
- 1/8 cup (30g) low-fat ricotta cheese
- 1/8 cup (30g) 0% fat greek yogurt
- 2 sun-dried tomatoes
- 4 black olives, halved
- 3-4 fresh basil leaves
- 1 tsp olive oil

Season tomatoes with halved olives, olive oil and basil. Let rest for 5-10 minutes. Spread bread with ricotta cheese and add tomatoes.

Serving size: 1 Total Fat: 7.9 g Saturated Fat: 1 g Trans Fat: 0 Calories: 214 Cholesterol: 7.2 mg Protein: 7 g Potassium: 145 mg Carbo: 28.6 g Fiber: 3.5 g Sugar: 3.4 g Sodium: 93.9 mg

Breakfast Burrito Recipe

30 min / 4 servings / Easy / Skillet - Wok

Ingredients:
- 8 oz (230g) cubed potatoes
- 12 oz (350g) chicken breast, cubed
- 1/4 cup (15g) chopped onion
- 1/2 cup (75g) red bell pepper, diced
- 3 oz (90g) fresh chopped spinach
- 1 eggs + 4 egg whites
- 1 garlic clove, chopped
- 1/2 cup (120g) 0% fat greek yogurt
- 4 Whole Wheat Tortillas (Dough Chapter)

Put in a wok the potatoes, garlic, cubed chicken, onion, spinach and pepper. Cook until meat and vegetables are ready. Add yogurt and eggs out of the fire and combine well. Divide and fill in 4 tortillas, folding in the sides over the filling and rolling, tucking in the edges as you go. Heat a skillet on medium heat, grease with spray oil, and cook for 3-4 minutes each side, covered.

Serving size. 1 filling+ 1 tortilla Total Fat: 8.7 g Satureted Fat: 7.1 g Trans Fat: 0 Calories: 385 Cholesterol: 46,5 mg Protein: 34.9 g Potassium: 157.6 mg Carbo: 41.5 g Fiber: 4.8 g Sugar: 3.5 g Sodium: 179,4 mg

Berry Cheesecake Parfait

20 min / 4 servings / Easy / Blender

Ingredients:
- 1. 1/2 cup (360g) 0% fat greek yogurt
- 2 oz (50g) low-fat cream cheese
- 2 tbsp granulated sugar
- 1 tsp vanilla extract
- 1 cup (150g) fresh blueberries
- 1 cup (150g) fresh strawberries

Place cream cheese, greek yogurt, sugar and vanilla into the blender. Blend the mixture until it is fluffy. Using 4 small glasses, make layers starting with strawberries and finishing with a little more cheese. Refrigerate until ready to serve.

Serving size: 1 Total Fat: 6.3 g Saturated Fat: 4 g Trans fat: 0 Calories: 167 Cholesterol: 23 mg Protein: 10 g Potassium: 86 mg Carbo: 17 g Fiber: 1.8 g Sugar: 16 g Sodium: 150 mg

Pumpkin Banana Bread Baked Oatmeal

60 min / 8 servings / Easy / Oven

Ingredients.

- 3 cups (240g) rolled oats
- 1 small (70g) mashed banana
- 1/2 cup (110g) pumpkin pureè
- 1/2 cup (100g) brown sugar
- 1 egg + 2 eggs whites
- 2 tsp baking powder
- 1 tsp cinnamon
- 1 tsp pumpkin spice
- 1 cup (240ml) skimmed milk
- 1 tsp vanilla extract
- 2 tbsp olive oil
- 1/3 cup (35g) chopped almonds

Preheat oven to 350° F.

Grease an 8x8 baking dish and set aside.

Combine oats, sugar, baking powder, salt, cinnamon, and pumpkin pie spice in a big bowl.

In a separate bowl, mix together pureè, banana, milk, vanilla, eggs, and oil. Pour the wet mix into the dry one and stir. Add almonds. Pour mixture into prepared baking dish.

Bake for 35-40 minutes or until golden.

Serving size: 1 Total Fat: 8.6 g Saturated fat: 1.4 g Trans fat: 0 Calories: 262 Cholesterol: 24 mg Protein: 8.2 g Potassium: 291 mg Carbo: 38 g Fiber: 5.6 g Sugar: 15 g Sodium: 176 mg

Homemade Super Easy Oatmeal Cookies

30 min / 25 cookies / Easy / Oven

Ingredients:

- 1 cup (80g) old-fashioned rolled oats
- 1 & 1/2 cups (170g) whole wheat flour
- 1/4 cup (50g) brown sugar
- 1 tbsp maple syrup
- 1/3 cup (40g) olive oil
- 1/4 cup (30g) chopped hazelnuts
- 1/4 cup (40g) raisins

In a bowl mix all ingredients.

Add little water if needed.

Roll out the dough onto a paper sheet and cut 25 cookies.

Bake at 400° F for about 20 minutes.

Serving size. 1 Total Fat: 3.9 g Saturated Fat: 0.6 g Trans Fat: 0 Calories: 83 Cholesterol: 23 mg Protein: 1.4 g Potassium: 86 mg Carbo: 10 g Fiber: 1.2 g Sugar: 3.5 g Sodium: 0.2 mg

Starbucks Pumpkin Scones Copycat Recipe

45 min / 18 servings / Medium / Oven

Ingredients

- 1/2 cup(110g) pumpkin pureè
- 2 egg whites
- 1/2 cup (125g) low-fat ricotta cheese
- 2 cups (260g) whole wheat flour
- 1/3 cup (65g) white sugar
- 1 tbsp baking powder
- 1 tsp ground cinnamon
- 1/2 tsp nutmeg
- 1/4 tsp ground ginger
- 1/4 tsp ground cloves

Glaze

- 2 cups (230g) powdered sugar
- 3 tbsp (45g) low-fat ricotta cheese
- 2 pinches ground cinnamon
- 1 pinch each of ground cloves and ground nutmeg

Preheat your oven to 375° F.

Combine the pumpkin pureè, egg and ricotta cheese with a fork and set aside. Combine in a separate bowl flour, sugar, baking powder, cinnamon, nutmeg, ginger and cloves, with a wire whisk. Pour pumpkin mixture into the flour and mix together gently with a spatula. Dump the dough onto a floured work surface and pick up half the dough. Fold it over the other half and continue until all the flour is incorporated. Create a round shape about 2 inches thick, and slice it into 10 triangular pieces. Bake on a baking paper sheet for about 20-23 minutes.

Combine powdered sugar with ricotta cheese until a thick glaze forms and divide in 2 bowls. In one bowl add cinnamon, cloves, and nutmeg and whisk to combine. Deep cold scones upside down into the white glaze. Let dry for 20 minutes. Pipe the spice glaze on top of the white to create a lined pattern. Allow the scones to sit for about 20 minutes so the glaze can harden.

Serving size: 1 Total Fat: 0.5 g Saturated Fat: 0.1 g Trans Fat: 0 Calories: 305 Cholesterol: 78.7 mg Protein: 25 g Potassium: 4.9 mg Carbo: 50 g Fiber: 2.1 g Sugar: 26.5 g Sodium: 382 mg

Light Oats Wholemeal Cookies

30 min / 25 cookies / Easy / Oven

Ingredients
- 2 cups (260g) whole wheat flour
- 2 cups (160g) old-fashioned rolled oats
- 1/2 cup (100g) brown sugar
- 1 tsp vanilla extract
- 2 tsp baking powder
- 1/3 (35ml) olive oil
- 1/4 (60ml) cup of water
- 1 lemon zest

Mix well all wet ingredients, then add flour and rolled oats, little by little. Work with your hands until the dough is ready. Add some water if needed. Roll out the dough onto a paper sheet and cut 25 cookies. Weat them a bit with water and bake for 20 minutes at 350° F.

Serving size: 1 Cookie Total Fat: 1.9 g Saturated Fat: 0.3 g Trans Fat: 0 Calorie: 86 Cholesterol: 0 mg Protein: 2.1 g Potassium: 51.7 mg Carbo: 15.2 g Fiber: 1.7 g Sugar: 4 g Sodium: 39.2 mg

Low-Sodium Low-Fat Doughs

Whole wheat tortillas

30 min / 6 servings / Easy / Fryer-pan

Ingredients:

- 1.8 cups (215g) whole wheat flour
- 1/2 cup (60g) plain flour
- 1 tsp baking powder
- 2 and 1/2 tbsp olive oil
- 1/8 cup (30ml) warm water

Combine all dry ingredients together, add oil and water little by little. Continue mixing until a smooth dough is formed. Divide into 6 pieces and roll them out thin.

Cook each tortilla for 2 minutes on each side, in a non-sticking fryer pan with spray oil.

Serving size: 1 Total Fat: 6.6 g Saturated Fat: 6.6 g Trans Fat: 0 Calories: 210 Cholesterol: 0 mg Protein: 5.4 g Potassium: 0.2 mg Carbo: 32 g Fiber: 3.3 g Sugar: 0.7 g Sodium: 81.3 mg

Bamboo Piadina

20 min / 8 servings / Easy / Fryer-pan

- 1/3 cup (100g) bamboo fiber (flour)
- 1/8 Psyllium (30g) husks flour
- 1 tsp (5g) Xanthan gum
- 1/8 (30g) cocco flour
- 1 tsp apple vinegar
- 1 tsp baking powder
- 1/3 (100gr) egg whites
- 1 and 1/2 cup (400ml) water

Combine all dry ingredients, add egg whites and water a little by little until a smooth dough is formed. Divide into 8 pieces and roll them out on a paper sheet. Cook each piadina for 2 minutes on each side in a non-sticking fryer-pan with spray oil.

Serving size: 1 Total Fat: 0.8 g Saturated Fat: 0 Trans fat: 0 Calories: 18 Cholesterol: 0 mg Protein: 2.1 g Potassium: 20 mg Carbo: 0 g Fiber: 16 g Sugar: 0 Sodium: 24.6 mg

Ricotta bread rolls

30 min / 6 servings / Easy / Oven

Ingredients

- 1/3 cup (80g) golden linseed flour (your food processor)
- 2 eggs
- 1/8 cup (30g) psyllium husks flour
- 1 tsp (5g) xanthan gum
- 2 tsp baking powder
- 1/2 cup l(100g)low-fat ricotta cheese

Mix all dry ingredients, then add ricotta and water if needed, until a smooth dough is formed. Bake in the oven, 375 degrees F. for 15-20 minutes.

Serving size: 1 Total Fat: 8 g Saturated Fat: 1.2 g Trans Fat: 0 Calories: 100 Cholesterol: 61 mg Protein: 5.8 g Potassium: 22 mg Carbo: 1.1 g Fiber: 4.9 g Sugar: 0.5 g Sodium: 52.7 mg

Almond flour bread rolls

1 hour / 6 servings / Medium / Oven

Ingredients

- 1/2 cup (50g) almond flour
- 1/8 cup (30g) psyllium husk flour
- 2 tsp baking powder
- 1 tsp apple vinegar
- 1 egg white
- 3/4 (255g) cup water

Preheat oven to 350° F. Mix all ingredients with electric beaters. Divide dough into pieces and make 6 little balls. With wet hands put them on a paper sheet and bake for 40-50 minutes.

Serving size: 1 Total Fat: 10 g Saturated Fat: 1 g Trans Fat: 0 Calories: 245 Cholesterol: 16 mg Protein: 5.3 g Potassium: 58 mg Carbo: 33 g Fiber: 3.2 g Sugar: 18 g Sodium: 91 mg

Rice Flour Shortbread Dough (gluten-free/ no butter)

10 min + 30 min rest / 6 servings / Easy

- 1 cup (135g) rice flour
- 1 cup (135g) potato starch
- 1/4 cup (37g) rice milk
- 1/4 cup (37g) sunflower oil
- 1/3 cup (65g) sugar
- 1 egg
- 1 tsp vanilla extract

Combine all wet ingredients, then add sugar and mix up. Mix together potato starch and rice flour, then add to wet ingredients. Work well until the dough is ready, using more rice flour if needed. Put in the fridge1 one hour before use.

Serving size: 1 Total Fat: 7.3 g Saturated Fat: 1.7 g Trans fat: 0 Calories: 265 Cholesterol: 31 mg Protein: 2.5 g Potassium: 11 mg Carbo: 47 g Fiber: 0 Sugar: 11 g Sodium: 11 g

Homemade Olive Oil Phyllo dough

1 hour / 1 phyllo sheet / Medium

- 1/3 cup (40g) whole wheat flour
- 1/8 cup (30ml) water
- 1 tbsp olive oil

Knead the ingredients until a soft dough is formed. Leave to rest for 10 minutes, then wrap it in plastic wrap and leave to rest at room temperature for about one hour. Roll out the dough into a 6-inch square using a rolling pin. Dust with flour. Roll again. You should wind up with a pastry that's 14x18 inches in size. If desired, you can roll it out more thinly.

Serving size: 1 sheet layer Total Fat: 5 g Saturated Fat: 1 g Trans Fat: 0 Calories: 197 Cholesterol: 0 Protein: 4.5 g Potassium: 46.9 mg Carbo: 33.4 g Fiber: 1g Sugar: 0 Sodium: 0.7 mg

Pie Crust Dough Recipe - double 9-inch pie pan recipe

30 Min / for a 10 servings pie / Easy

Ingredients

- 2 1/2 cups (325g) whole wheat flour
- 3 tbsp granulated erythritol

- 1/2 cup (65g) olive oil
- 1/4 cup (60g) cold water

Add in a bowl flour, erythritol, and oil to form crumbs. Add cold water and form a ball. Refrigerate for about 30 minutes, then divide the dough into 2 pieces and roll each one out with a rolling pin, having your dough between 2 parcel sheets.

Serving size: 1 (just the pie crust of your pie) Total Fat: 12 g Saturated Fat: 1.1 g Trans Fat: 0 Calories: 210 Cholesterol: 0 Protein: 4 g Potassium: 109 mg Carbo: 21.6 g Fiber: 3.3 g Sugar: 0 Sodium: 0.5 mg

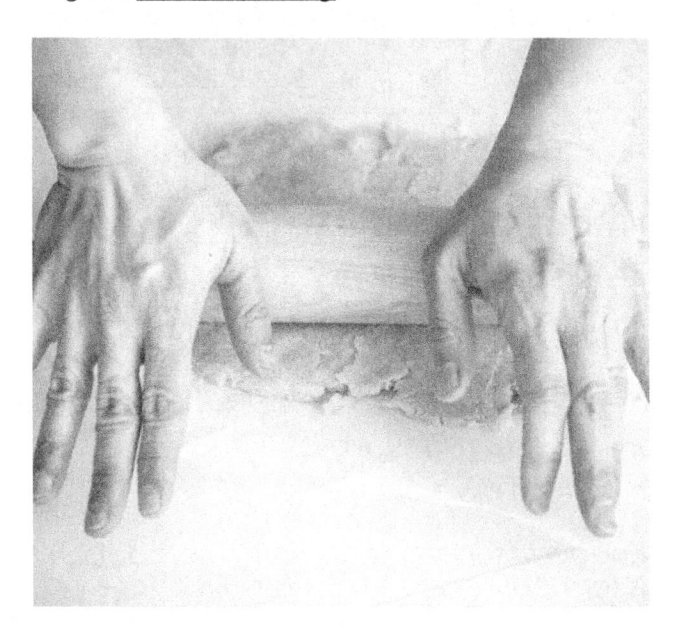

Easy Flaky Oil Pie Crust (for sweet and savory fillings)

9-inch pie pan - 2 sheet

20 mins / 8 servings / Easy / Oven

Ingredients

- 3 cups (375g) whole wheat flour
- 3/4 cup (100ml) olive oil
- 1/3 cup (80ml) skimmed milk

Whisk flour with oil and milk and stir all together. If the dough seems too dry, add 1-2 tbsp of milk more. When the dough starts to form, finish working gently.

Divide into 2 parts and roll each piece out between two parcel sheets. Remove the top one and use the bottom one to lift and flip the dough onto the pie plate and on top of the filling. Trim and seal edges. Cut some slits for ventilation. Bake in a preheated oven at 425° F for 15 minutes, then bake at 375° F until the crust is golden and the filling is cooked. Usually about another 30-45 minutes.

Serving size: 1 Total Fat: 23.1 g Saturated Fat: 3.5 g Trans Fat: 0 Calories: 365 Cholesterol: 0 Protein: 6.3 g Potassium: 163.5 mg Carbo: 32.9 g Fiber: 4.9 g Sugar: 0.5 g Sodium: 5.1 mg

Olive Oil Tart Crust 9-inch pie pan recipe (no rolling pin)

30 mins / for a 6 servings pie / Easy

Ingredients

- 1 1/2 cups (135g) whole wheat flour
- 4 tbsp (60ml) extra virgin olive oil
- 3 tbsp cold water
- Pepper if you like it

Add water to oil in a glass and set aside. Pour flour in a bowl, add pepper and oil mix and drizzle over the flour mixture. Whisk with a fork untill the dough is sandy. Add more water if needed, it should hold together when you pinch a small piece between your fingers. Press the dough into the bottom and up the sides of your pan.

Serving size: 1 Total Fat: 10.1 g Saturated Fat: 1.6 g Trans Fat: 0 Calories: 193 Cholesterol: 0 Protein: 4 g Potassium: 109 mg Carbo: 21.6 g Fiber: 3.3 g Sugar: 0 Sodium: 0.5 mg

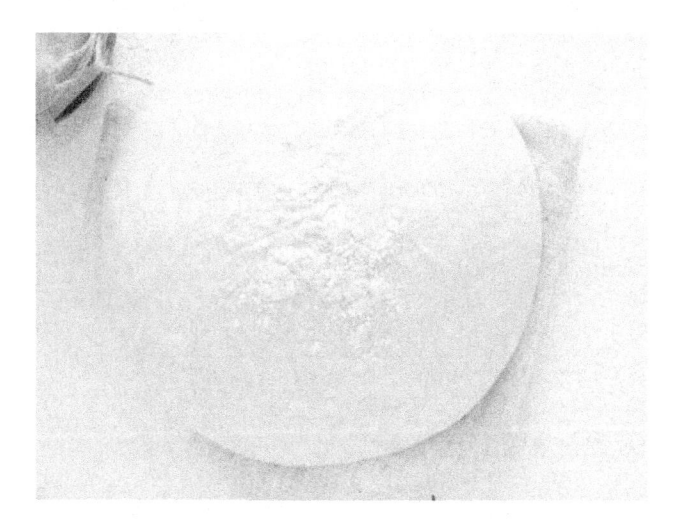

Italian Homemade Family Wholemeal Pizza Dough

20 mins / 8 servings / Super Easy

Ingredients

- 4 cups (500g) whole wheat flour
- 3 tbsp extra virgin olive oil
- 1 & 1/3 cups (320ml) warm water
- 1 tsp (6-7g) brewer's yeast
- 1/2 tsp sugar

Pour flour into a large bowl. Dissolve yeast in the warm water and add to the flour at one time. Whisk with a fork, bringing the flour to the center of the bowl. Knead for a short time, just until all flour is well taken and the dough is very soft. Seal the bowl with food plastic wrap. Put the bowl in the turned-off oven for 2 hours, then put the bowl into the fridge for 10-12 hours at a temperature of 7–8 degrees. Take the dough out of the fridge and leave it for at least one hour so that it reaches room temperature before use.

Serving size: 1 Total Fat: 9.5 g Saturated Fat: 2.1 g Trans Fat: 0 Calories: 593 Cholesterol: 0 Protein: 46.9 g Potassium: 245 mg Carbo: 79.9 g Fiber: 26.6 g Sugar: 0.3 g Sodium: 1 mg

Low-Sodium Homemade Seasonings

Taco Seasoning Spices Mix

Ingredients
- 4 tbsp chili powder
- 6 tsp ground cumin
- 4 tsp paprika
- 1 tsp garlic powder
- 1 tsp onion powder
- 1 tsp dried oregano
- 1/4 tsp of red pepper flakes

Mix together all ingredients and store in a sealed jar.

Garam Masala Homemade Mix

Ingredients
- 1 tsp dried cumin
- 1 tsp dried coriander
- 1 tsp dried cardamom
- 1 tsp dried cinnamon
- 1/2 tsp dried garlic
- 1/2 tsp nutmeg
- 1 pinch of pepper

Mix together all ingredients and store in a sealed jar.

Jamaican Jerk Seasoning Mix

Ingredients
- 1 tsp garlic powder
- 1 tsp onion powder
- 1 tsp cayenne pepper
- 1 tsp brown sugar
- 1 tsp dried thyme
- 1 tsp ground black pepper
- 1 tsp paprika
- 1 tsp dried parsley
- 1/2 tsp ground nutmeg
- 1/2 tsp cumin
- 1/2 tsp ground cinnamon

Mix together all ingredients and store in a sealed jar.

Steak Seasoning Mix

Ingredients
- 1 tbsp cayenne
- 1 tbsp onion powder
- 1/2 tbsp garlic powder
- 1 tbs paprika
- 1/2 tbsp brown sugar
- 1 tsp cumin
- 1 tsp mustard powder
- 1 tsp tumeric
- 1 tsp pepper

Mix together all ingredients and store in a sealed jar.

Fajita Seasoning Mix

Ingredients
- 1 tsp cayenne powder
- 1 tsp paprika
- 1/2 tsp garlic powder
- 1 tsp onion powder
- 1 tsp dried oregano
- 1/2 tsp brown sugar
- 1/2 tsp cumin

Mix together all ingredients and store in a sealed jar

Gather up your ingredients and simply mix them all together in a small bowl. Make sure they are well combined. Store them in a sealed jar for up to 6 months, but they start to lose their flavor after a few months. So it is best to make smaller batches of seasonings at a time.

Low-Sodium Low-Fat Soups

Tuscany "Ribollita" italian recipe

2 hours + 5 hours rest / 6 servings / Medium

Ingredients

- 2 & 1/2 cups (200g) black cabbage
- 2 cups of (180g) green cabbage
- 1 can 15 oz low sodium cannellini beans (400g)
- 1 onion
- 2 carrots
- 1 & 1/2 cups (125g) of potatoes, diced
- 1tsp fresh sage
- 1 tbsp tomato sauce
- 4 tbsp extra virgin olive oil
- 4 crusty bread slices (200g all)

In a large pot saute onion and olive oil for 2 minutes, add carrots and potatoes cubed very little and cook for about 4-5 minutes. Add black and green cabbages sliced, sage, and tomato, and cook slowly for about 1 hour. Add beans and let it cook for 20 minutes. Place bread slices in a crackpot and add all vegetable soup. Rest for 4-5 hours before serving.

Serving size: 1 Total Fat: 4.9 g _Saturated Fat: 1 g_ Trans Fat: 0 _Calories: 247 Cholesterol: 0_ Protein: 10 g Potassium: 462 mg Carbo: 40 g Fiber: 7.9 g Sugar: 2.4 g _Sodium: 221 mg_

Harvest Pumpkin Soup

30 mins / 2 servings / Easy

Ingredients

- 1 pound (450g) fresh pumpkin
- 1 tbsp olive oil
- 1 garlic cloves
- 1 tbsp fresh parsley, chopped

Wash the pumpkin well and cut into 1-inch cubes. In a saucepan saute olive oil and garlic cloves for 2 minutes. Add pumpkin cubes, parsley, and water to cover them. Cook on medium-high heat for 20 minutes. Using an immersion blender, purée mixture until smooth.

Serving size: 1 Total Fat: 7.3 g Saturated Fat: 1 g Trans Fat: 0 Calories: 136 Cholesterol: 0 Protein: 2.4 g Potassium: 781 mg Carbo: 15.3 g Fiber: 2.3 g Sugar: 2.3 g Sodium: 3.8 mg

Creamy Mushroom Soup

40 mins / 5 servings / Easy

Ingredients

- 1 pound (450g) fresh champignon mushrooms, sliced
- 1 onion, chopped
- 1 garlic clove, minced
- 2 tbsp olive oil
- 1 tbsp fresh parsley, chopped
- 3 tbsp cornstarch
- 4 cups skimmed milk
- 1 tbsp balsamic vinegar

Heat oil over medium heat in a large saucepan, add onion and mushrooms and cook for about 10 minutes. Add vinegar, garlic and parsley and cook for 3-4 minutes. In a little bowl mix cornstarch with milk, then add it to the saucepan. Bring to a boil, cook, and stir until thickened, 5-6 minutes.

Serving size: 1 Total Fat: 5.6 g Saturated Fat: 0.8 g Trans Fat: 0 Calories: 162 Cholesterol: 3.2 mg Protein: 7.8 g Carbo: 19.9 g Fiber: 1 g Sugar: 11.4 g Sodium: 102.6 mg

Chunky Vegetable Lentil Soup

30 mins / 2 servings / Easy

Ingredients

- 1 cup (240ml) low sodium vegetable broth
- 1/2 cup (65g) carrots, diced
- 2 tomatoes, diced
- 1 cup (200g) dry lentils
- 1 garlic clove, minced
- 1 tsp fresh parsley, chopped
- 1 tbsp celery, slided
- 1 tbsp extra virgin olive oil

Add all ingredients to a large pot, add 1 cup of water, and cook on a medium heat for 15-16 minutes.

Serving size: 1 Total Fat: 7.1 g Saturated Fat: 1 g Trans Fat: 0 Calories: 344 Cholesterol: 0 Protein: 18.2 g Potassium: 305 mg Carbo: 51.8 g Fiber: 21.8 g Sugar: 7.4 g Sodium: 315 mg

Curried Mushrooms and Cauliflower Soup

40 mins / 4 servings / Easy

Ingredients

- 1 pound (450g) raw cauliflower, cut into florets
- 1 pound (450g) mushrooms, sliced
- 1 tbsp celery chopped
- 1 tbsp onion, chopped,
- 1 tbsp fresh parsley
- 1 carrot, sliced
- 1 potato, chopped
- 2 tbsp extra virgin olive oil
- 2 cups (480 ml) low sodium vegetable broth
- 2 cups (480 ml)water
- 1/2 tsp curry powder

In a large pot saute oil, onion, celery and parsley for 2 minutes. Add potatoes and carrots and saute for 2 minutes more. Add cauliflower, mushrooms, curry, broth, and water. Stir and let simmer for 5-7 minutes or until cauliflower and mushrooms have cooked down. Serve and garnish with plenty of cilantro.

Serving size: 1 Total Fat: 7.3 g Saturated Fat: 1 g Trans Fat: 0 Calories: 151 Cholesterol: 0 Protein: 7.1 g Potassium: 143 mg Carbo: 14.4 g Fiber: 8 g Sugar: 5.9 g Sodium: 89.8 mg

Beef and Barley Soup

10 mins + cooking time 2 hours / 3 servings / Medium

Ingredients

- 1 pound (450g)stewing beef, cubed
- 1 tbsp olive oil
- 1 clove garlic, minced
- 1 rib celery, diced
- 1 carrot, diced
- 2 tbsp onion, diced
- 1 cup (240ml) homemade unsalted vegetables broth
- 3 cups (720 ml) of water
- 1/2 cup (85g) pearl barley
- 1 tbsp fresh parsley, minced

Add into a large heavy pot onion, celery, garlic and carrot. Saute for 3-4 minutes, Add broth, parsley and meat. Once boiling turn the heat down to a simmer. Simmer for 45 minutes partially covered. Add the barley and simmer until tender (50-60 minutes).

Serving size: 1 Total Fat: 12 g Saturated Fat: 3.3 g Trans Fat: 0 Calories: 333 Cholesterol: 97.3 mg Protein: 36.6 g Carbo: 20.5 g Fiber: 4.3 g Sugar: 2 g Sodium: 235 mg

Broccoli Cheese Soup

30 mins / 3 servings / Easy

Ingredients

- 1 tbsp white onion, chopped
- 1 tbsp extra virgin olive oil
- 1 tbsp celery, chopped
- 1 tbsp carrot, chopped
- 9 cups (450g) broccoli, chopped
- 3 cups (720ml) water
- 2 cups (280g) raw cashews (soak overnight in water)
- 2 cups skimmed milk

Saute in a large saucepan oil, onion, carrot and celery for 3-4 minutes. Add broccoli and water and bring to a simmer for 5-6 minutes. In a blender add cashews and milk and blend on high speed until smooth and creamy and add to broccoli. Bring to a simmer and start stirring to combine. Your soup will be ready in 3-4 minutes more.

Serving size: 1 Total Fat: 41 g Saturated Fat: 0.7 g Trans Fat: 0 Calories: 584 Cholesterol: 0 Protein: 26.8 g Carbo: 26.8 g Fiber: 9 g Sugar: 19.8 g Sodium: 77.1 mg

Stuffed Pepper Soup

1 hour / 3 servings / Medium

Ingredients

- 8 oz (240g) ground beef
- 1 tbsp olive oil
- 1 red bell pepper, diced
- 2 tbsp onion, diced
- 1/2 jalapeño, seeds and ribs removed, minced
- 2 cups (480ml) low sodium vegetable broth
- 1/2 can (7 oz-200g) tomato sauce
- 1 can (15 oz-400g) diced peeled tomatoes
- 1 tbsp maple syrup
- 1 cup (185g) raw long grain rice, uncooked
- 1 tbsp cilantro for garnish

Heat oil in a large saucepan. Add onion and jalapeño and saute for 2 minutes. Add meat and bell pepper untill meat is cooked, about 7-8 minutes. Add rice, broth, tomato sauce, peeled tomatoes and syrup. Bring to a simmer stirring often. Simmer for 30 minutes. Serve with parsley on top.

Serving size: 1 Total Fat: 14.7 g Saturated Fat: 4.2 g Trans Fat: 0 Calories: 492 Cholesterol: 54.2 mg Protein: 23.9 g Potassium: 370.2 mg Carbo: 66.1 g Fiber: 4 g Sugar: 12.3 g Sodium: 226.3 mg

Turkey Long Grain Rice Soup

1 hour 30 / 2 servings / Medium

Ingredients

- 10 oz (290g) turkey breast, cubed
- 1/2 cup (90g)long grain rice, uncooked
- 1 tbsp olive oil
- 1 onion, chopped
- 1 carrot, chopped
- 1 stalk celery, chopped

- 1 tbsp whole wheat flou
- 1 cup (240ml) skimmed milk
- 1/3 (80ml) cup water
- 1 tsp basil leaves, chopped
- 1/2 tsp fresh rosemary
- 1 tbsp fresh parsley, chopped

In a large soup pot heat olive oil over medium-high heat, then add the turkey and cook for about 5 to 7 minutes. Remove the turkey from the pot and set aside.

Add onion, carrots and celery in the same pot and cook for about 3 minutes. Add flour and whisk well. Add milk, rice and water, bring to a boil and cover. Cook on medium-low for about 30-32 minutes or until rice is ready. Add basil, parsley, rosemary and the turkey back to the pot.

Cook for 3-4 minutes more. Serve hot.

Serving size: 1 Total Fat: 8.2 g Saturated Fat: 2.4 g Trans Fat: 0 Calories: 432 Cholesterol: 70 mg Protein: 42.5 g Potassium: 787.8 mg Carbo: 47 g Fiber: 2 g Sugar: 8.5 g Sodium: 173.3 mg

Dairy-Free Chicken Pot Pie Soup

50 mins / 4 servings / Medium

Ingredients

- 12 oz (350g) boneless skinless chicken breasts, cut into 1-inch pieces
- 2 tbsp extra virgin olive oil
- 1 small onion, diced,
- 2 tbsp whole wheat flour
- 1 cup (240ml) low-sodium vegetable broth
- 2 cups (480ml) skimmed milk
- 1 cup (160g) fresh corn
- 1 cup (128g) fresh carrot, chopped
- 1 cup (145g) fresh or frozen peas
- 1 cup (230g) boiled beans
- 2 toasted whole wheat bread slices 1-inch (150g)

In a large dutch oven add 1 tbsp of oil and chicken and cook, stirring occasionally, until it is mostly cooked. Transfer to a plate and set aside leaving the juices in the pot.

In the same dutch oven add 1 tbsp of oil and onion and cook for 3.4 minutes. Add flour and stir to combine, then add broth, little by little, preventing clumps. Continue cooking until the mixture has thickened, about 3-5 minutes. Add milk and vegetables, stir to combine, cover and let simmer on low heat for 12-15 minutes. Add the 2 toasted french bread, broken in 3-4 pieces each, to the soup.

Transfer the pot to the oven and bake for 15-20 minutes.

Serving size: 1 Total Fat: 10.7 g Saturated Fat: 1 g Trans Fat: 0 Calories: 434 Cholesterol: 0 Protein: 30.5 g Potassium: 515.9 mg Carbo: 53.9 g Fiber: 719.5 g Sugar: 18.1 g Sodium: 358 mg

Low-Sodium Low-Fat Pasta

Healthy Shrimps Spaghetti Italian Style

30 mins / 2 servings / Easy / Skillet

Ingredients
- 8 oz (230g) deveined shrimps
- 1 cup (150g) cherry tomatoes
- 1 garlic clove
- 1 tbsp extra virgin olive oil
- 1 tbsp fresh parsley, chopped
- pepper to taste
- 5 oz (140g) whole wheat dry spaghetti

Bring a pot of water to a boil. In a large skillet heat oil on medium-high heat, add garlic and saute for 1-2 minutes. Then add halved cherry tomatoes and cook for 2-3 minutes, turning them with a spoon. Add spaghetti to boiling water and stir with a fork. Add shrimps to tomatoes and cook just 1 to 2 minutes per side until opaque and cooked through, stirring well. Turn the heat off and wait for the pasta. Spaghetti must be cooked 2-3 minutes less than their cooking time. Drain the spaghetti and add to the shrimp. Heat skillet on medium-high heat and toss until spaghetti are ready. Serve with fresh parsley sprinkled on top.

Serving size: 1 Total Fat: 8.4 g Saturated Fat: 1 Trans Fat: 0 Calories: 373 Cholesterol: 0 Protein: 24.4 g Potassium: 193 mg Carbo: 49.9 g Fiber: 7,3 g Sugar: 4,5 g Sodium: 5 mg

Catfish & Cherry Tomatoes Pasta

20 mins / 2 servings / Easy / Skillet

Ingredients

- 6 oz (170g) catfish fillet
- 10 oz (280g) cherry tomatoes halved
- 1 tbsp fresh parsley chopped
- 1 garlic clove, halved
- 1 tbs extra virgin olive oil
- 5 oz (140g) whole wheat dry penne rigate

Heat a pot of water to a boil. Cut the fillet into pieces. In a large skillet heat oil on medium heat and add garlic. Saute for 1-2 minutes, add fish and saute for 2 minutes. Add halved cherry tomatoes and cook for 3-4 minutes more, stirring gently. Add penne to boiling water. The cooking time is 2-3 minutes less than cooking instruction. Drain pasta and add to the catfish sauce. Heat skillet on medium-high heat and toss until ready.

Serve with fresh parsley sprinkled on top.

Serving size: 1 Total Fat: 16,9 g Saturated Fat: 1 g Trans Fat: 0 Calories: 435 Cholesterol: 0 mg Protein: 23 g Potassium: 16.5 mg Carbo: 47,7 g Fiber: 8,8 g Sugar: 6,7 g Sodium: 1,5 mg

Sicilian Ricotta & Pistachios Penne Rigate

20 mins / 2 servings / Super Easy / Skillet

Ingredients

- 5 oz (140g) low fat ricotta cheese
- 1 oz (28g) shelled unsalted pistachios
- 1 tbsp extra virgin olive oil
- 1 garlic clove
- 1/2 cup (120ml) skimmed milk
- 1 tbsp fresh basil, chopped
- 6 oz (170g) whole wheat dry penne rigate

Start a pot of water to a boil. Pour pistachios into the food processor, pulse 4-5 times and set aside. In a large skillet pan heat oil to medium heat, add garlic and saute for 1-2 minutes. Add milk, pistachios and ricotta cheese and whisk until well combined. Cook for 2-3 minutes and turn the heat off. Add pasta to boiling water. The cooking time is 2-3 minutes less than the instructions. Drain the penne and add to the ricotta sauce immediately. Heat to medium-high heat and saute pasta, stirring with a wooden spoon for 2-3 minutes.

Serve with fresh chopped basil on top.

Serving size: 1 Total Fat: 20.7 g Saturated Fat: 5.8 g Trans Fat: 0 Calories: 542 Cholesterol: 18.8 mg Protein: 22.5 g Potassium: 207 mg Carbo: 66.3 g Fiber: 11 g Sugar: 7.2 g Sodium: 206.1 mg

Orecchiette Pasta with Broccoli Florets

20 mins / 2 servings / Easy / Skillet

Ingredients

- 3 cups (270g) raw broccoli florets
- 2 tbsp extra virgin olive oil
- 2 garlic cloves, sliced
- 5 oz (140g) whole wheat dry orecchiette
- 2 tbsp grated parmesan cheese

Bring a pot of water to a boil. Heat a large skillet on medium heat, add olive oil and sliced garlic cloves and saute for 1-2 minutes. Add broccoli and 1 cup of water to the skillet, cover, and simmer for 3-4 minutes, stirring occasionally. Taste broccoli and when ready, continue cooking without a lid for 3-4 minutes more or until broccoli is very tender and water is half absorbed. Add pasta to the boiling water and drain 2-3 minutes before cooking time. Add pasta immediately to the skillet, heat on medium-high heat, and saute pasta and broccoli for 2 minutes, stirring continuously.

Serve with grated parmesan on top.

Serving size: 1 Total Fat: 18,2 g Saturated Fat: 3 g Trans Fat: 0 Calories: 430 Cholesterol: 5,5 mg Protein: 15,6 g Potassium: 20 mg Carbo: 51 g Fiber: 8 g Sugar: 2,5 g Sodium: 126,5 mg

Creamy Zucchini Sauce Fusilli

20 mins / 2 servings / Easy / Food Processor

Ingredients

- 5 oz (140g) whole wheat dry fusilli
- 12 oz (340g) fresh zucchini, diced
- 3 oz (85g) low fat ricotta cheese
- 2 tbsp extra virgin olive oil
- 1 tbsp fresh parsley, chopped
- 1 garlic clove, chopped
- 2 tbsp grated parmesan cheese

Bring a pot of water to a boil. Blend diced zucchini in a food processor until smooth and creamy and set aside. Heat a large skillet pan to medium heat, add oil and garlic and saute for 1-2 minutes, add zucchini cream and simmer for 2-3 minutes stirring. Add ricotta and parsley and mix well and set aside. Add pasta to boiling water and drain 2-3 minutes before cooking time. Add immediately to zucchini cream, heat the skillet to medium heat and saute pasta for 1-2 minutes. Top with grated parmesan cheese.

Serving size:1 Total Fat: 21g Saturated Fat: 5.3 g Trans Fat: 0 Calories: 451 Cholesterol: 16.8 mg Protein: 18.5 g Potassium: 804.8 mg Carbo: 47 g Fiber: 6.4 g Sugar: 1 g Sodium: 165.9 mg

Chicken & Black Kale Pasta Skillet

30 mins / 2 servings / Easy / Skillet

- 5 oz (140g) whole wheat dry penne
- 6 oz (170g) chicken breast, cubed
- 6 oz (170g) raw black kale, chopped
- 7 oz (200g) boiled cannellini beans
- 1 tbsp extra virgin olive oil
- 1 garlic clove, chopped
- 1 tbsp fresh basil, chopped

Heat a large skillet on medium heat, add oil, chicken and garlic and saute for 2 minutes. Add kale and 2 cups of water, cover skillet and cook 10-12 minutes. Add beans, and more water for pasta and bring to a boil. Add pasta and cook simmering continuously until pasta is ready. Serve with basil spread on top.

Serving size: 1 Total Fat: 9.8 g Saturated Fat: 1 g Trans Fat: 0 Calories: 515 Cholesterol: 0 Protein: 40 g Potassium: 715 mg Carbo: 66.6 g Fiber: 15.5 g Sugar: 5.5 g Sodium: 35.5 mg

Cauliflower & Peas Pasta

30 mins / 2 servings / Easy / Stove pot

- 5 oz (140g) whole wheat dry ditalini
- 9 oz (225g) cauliflower, chopped
- 1 cup (160g) frozen peas
- 2 tbsp extra virgin olive oil
- 1 garlic clove, halved
- 2 tbsp grated parmesan
- 1 tbsp fresh parsley, chopped

Add in a stove pot cauliflower, peas, parsley, garlic, and 2-3 cups of water (you have to cover vegetables plus 2 inches of water to cook pasta) and bring to a boil. Let vegetables cook for about 20 minutes, then add pasta to the pot and stir. Serve topped with grated parmesan cheese.

Serving size: 1 Total Fat: 17.6 g Saturated Fat: 3 g Trans Fat: 0 Calories: 471 Cholesterol: 5.5 mg Protein: 17.4 g Potassium: 24.5 mg Carbo: 60.8 g Fiber: 2.7 g Sugar: 6.4 g Sodium: 97 mg

Lentil & Celery Ditalini Pasta

20 mins / 2 servings / Easy / Stove-Pot

Ingredients

- 5 oz (140g) whole wheat dry ditalini
- 3/4 cup (150g) dry lentils
- 1/2 cup (55g) sliced celery
- 1 tbsp extra virgin olive oil
- 1 garlic clove
- 2 cherry tomatoes, halved
- 1 tbsp fresh parsley, chopped

In a large pot add all ingredients plus 3 cups (720ml) of water and bring to a boil. Let lentils simmer for about 15-16 minutes, then add ditalini pasta and continue cooking on medium heat as instructions. Serve hot.

Serving size: 1 Total Fat: 8.9 g Saturated Fat: 1 g Trans Fat: 0 Calories: 461 Cholesterol: 0 Protein: 21.2 g Potassium: 244.5 mg Carbo: 74 g Fiber: 14.5 g Sugar: 1.5 g Sodium: 71.5 mg

Tomato & Basil Caprese Pasta Salade

20 minutes / 2 servings / Easy / Stove pot

Ingredients

- 5 oz (140g) whole wheat dry penne
- 12 oz (340g) halved cherry tomatoes
- 3 oz (85g) part-skim mozzarella cheese (chunk package), cubed
- 10 fresh basil leaves
- 2 tbsp extra virgin olive oil

Bring a pot of water to a boil. Add pasta and cook as cooking instructions, taste it before draining. When pasta is ready, drain it well and rinse it with cold water. Add cold pasta to a bowl, add tomatoes, mozzarella, basil leaves and oil and mix..

Serving size: 1 Total Fat: 22.9 g Saturated Fat: 6.5 g Trans Fat: 0 Calories: 516 Cholesterol: 27 mg Protein: 21.6 g Potassium: 39 mg Carbo: 56 g Fiber. 8.3 g Sugar: 8.4 g Sodium: 262.5 mg

Fresh Salmon Fettuccine Skillet

20 mins / 2 servings / Easy / Skillet

Ingredients

- 5 oz (140g) whole wheat dry fusilli
- 5 oz (140g) fresh salmon fillet
- 1/2 cup (120g) 0% fat greek yogurt
- 2 tbsp extra virgin olive oil
- 1 garlic clove, chopped
- 1 tbsp onion, chopped
- 1 tbsp fresh parsley, chopped

Bring a pot of water to a boil. Cut salmon fillet into little cubes and set aside. Heat a large skillet on medium heat, add oil, garlic and onion and saute for 2 minutes. Add salmon cubes and cook for 4-5 minutes stirring occasionally. Turn off the heat, and add yogurt and chopped parsley. Add fusilli pasta to the boiling water and stir. Cook for 2 minutes less than instructions. Drain pasta and add immediately to the salmon sauce. Heat the skillet on medium heat and saute pasta 2 minutes stirring continuously. Serve immediately.

Serving size: 1 Total Fat: 23.4 g Saturated Fat: 2 g Trans Fat: 0 Calorie: 487 Cholesterol: 0 Protein: 26.1 g Potassium: 16.5 mg Carbo: 43 g Fiber: 4.7 g Sugar: 1.5 g Sodium: 1.5 mg

Red Bell Pepper Macaroni

30 min / 2 servings / Easy / Skillet

Ingredients

- 5 oz (140g) whole wheat dry macaroni pasta
- 10 oz (280g) red bell pepper, diced
- 2 tbsp extra virgin olive oil
- 1 garlic clove, chopped
- 1 onion chopped
- 4-5 fresh basil leaves
- 4 cherry tomatoes, halved

Bring a pot of water to a boil. Heat a large skillet pan on medium-high heat, add garlic and onion and saute for 2-3 minutes, then add cherry tomatoes and red bell pepper and saute for 13-15 minutes, stirring occasionally. 2-3 minutes before turning off heat add 1/2 cup of water (120ml) and bring to a boil on high heat. Add macaroni to the boiling water and drain 2-3 minutes before instruction time. Add immediately to the skillet. Heat on medium-high heat and saute for 2-3 minutes, stirring continuously. Serve with chopped basil on top.

Serving size: 1 Total Fat: 15.5 g Saturated Fat: 2.7 g Trans Fat: 0 Calories: 406 Cholesterol: 0 Protein: 10.4 g Potassium: 69.5 mg Carbo: 56.2 g Fiber: 8.2 g Sugar: 9.2 g Sodium: 50.6 mg

Walnuts & Basil Penne

15 mins / 2 servings / Super Easy

- 5 oz (140g) whole wheat dry penne
- 1/2 cup (75g) chopped walnuts
- 3 tbsp fresh basil, chopped
- 1 tbsp extra virgin olive oil

Bring a pot of water to a boil. Mix walnuts, oil and basil in a big bowl. Cook and pour pasta into the bowl. Serve immediately.

Serving size: 1 Total Fat: 27.8 g Saturated Fat: 3 g Trans Fat 0 Calories: 485 Cholesteerol: 0 Protein: 13 g Potassium: 8 mg Carbo: 47 g Fiber: 6.7 g Sugar: 2.9 g Sodium: 0

Spinach & Ricotta Spaghetti

20 mins / 2 servings / Easy / Food processor

Ingredients

- 5 oz (140g) whole wheat dry spaghetti
- 7 oz (200g) fresh chopped spinach
- 3 oz (85g) low fat ricotta cheese
- 1 tbsp fresh onion, chopped
- 1 tbsp extra virgin olive oil
- 2 tbsp grated parmesan cheese

Blend spinach in the food processor until smooth and creamy. Bring a pot of water to a boil. Heat a large skillet pan on medium heat, add oil, 1 cup of water and spinach cream and cook for 4-5 minutes, stirring occasionally. Add ricotta and mix well. Turn off the heat. Add spaghetti to the boiling water and cook for 2 minutes less than cooking instructions time. Before draining spaghetti keep apart 2 cups (240ml) of water. Drain spaghetti and add to the spinach cream. Heat the skillet on medium heat and mix. Add some water if needed. Serve hot with grated parmesan on top.

Serving size. 1 Total Fat: 13.8 g Saturated Fat: 4.3 g Trans Fat: 0 Calories: 406 Cholesterol: 16.8 mg Protein: 18.3 g Carbo: 52.8 g Fiber: 8.3 g Sugar: 3 g Sodium: 238 mg

One-Pot Meat Sauce Pasta Recipe

30 mins / 2 servings / Easy / Stove-pot

Ingredients

- 5 oz (140g) whole wheat dry penne rigate pasta
- 7 oz (200g) ground beef 90% lean
- 10 oz (300g) tomatoes, diced
- 1 small carrot, chopped
- 1 celery stick, chopped
- 1 tbsp fresh basil, chopped
- 1 tbsp extra virgin olive oil
- 1 garlic clove, chopped
- 1 tbsp onion, chopped

Heat a large stove pot on medium-high heat. Add oil, garlic, onion, carrot, and celery and cook for 3-4 minutes, stirring occasionally. Add ground beef, mash it with a fork and saute for 2-3 minutes. Add tomatoes and 1 cup (240ml) of water and stir. Low heat on low- medium and keep on cooking for 20 minutes. Bring a little stove pot with 2 cups of water (480ml) to a boil in case you need sauce. Add pasta to the sauce and cook for the instructions time, stirring occasionally. (add hot water from the other stove pot if pasta is too sticky) Serve immediately.

Serving size: 1 Total Fat: 17.8 g Saturated Fat: 5 g Trans Fat: 0 Calories: 509 Cholesterol: 65 mg Protein: 29.7 g Potassium: 411 mg Carbo: 57.6 g Fiber: 12.7 g Sugar: 7.4g Sodium: 88.6 mg

Eggplant & Ricotta Rigatoni

30 mins / 2 servings Easy / Microwave

Ingredients

- 10 oz (280g) eggplants
- 5 oz (140g) whole wheat dry rigatoni
- 2 tbsp extra virgin olive oil
- 1/2 cup (120g) low fat ricotta cheese
- 4-5 fresh basil leaves, chopped
- 2 garlic cloves, chopped
- 4-5 cherry tomatoes, halved

Cut eggplants into slices and slices into strips.

Lay eggplant strips on a microwave crisper pan and microwave for 10 minutes (crisp function).

Heat a skillet pan on medium heat, add oil and garlic and saute for 1-2 minutes.

Add eggplant strips and saute for 3-4 minutes, add halved cherry tomatoes and saute for 3-4 minutes more.

Add rigatoni to the boiling water and drain 2-3 minutes before instruction time. Add immediately to the mix, heat on medium-high heat and saute rigatoni for 2-3 minutes, stirring continuously. Turn off the heat and add ricotta cheese with a spoon, stirring just 2-3 times. Serve immediately.

Serving size: 1 Total Fat: 19 g Saturated Fat: 4 g Trans Fat: 0 Calorie: 469 Cholesterol: 20 mg Protein: 17 g Potassium: 397 mg Carbo: 56 g Fiber: 11 g Sugar: 6.6 g Sodium: 155 mg

Artichokes and black olives Fettuccine

30 mins / 2 servings / Easy

Ingredients

- 2 cups (170g) artichoke hearts
- 5 oz (140g) whole wheat dry fettuccine
- 1/2 cup (80g) black olives, sliced
- 2 garlic cloves, halved
- 1 celery stick, sliced
- 2 tbsp fresh parsley, chopped
- 1 tbsp extra virgin olive oil

Heat a large skillet on medium-high heat. Add artichoke hearts, garlic, oil, celery, sliced olives, and 2 cups (480ml) of water and cook for 12-13 minutes. When artichokes are more than halfway ready add pasta to boiling water and cook 3-4 minutes less than instructions. Drain fettuccine and add immediately to artichokes, add water if needed. Continue to cook until pasta is ready. Spread chopped parsley and serve immediately.

Serving size: 1 Total fat: 12.4 g _Saturated Fat: 1 g_ Trans Fat: 0 _Calories: 449 Cholesterol: 0_ Protein: 15.1g Potassium: 33 mg Carbo: 69 g Fiber: 13 g Sugar: 11.3 g _Sodium: 169mg_

Low-Sodium Low-Fat Vegetables and Salads

Tomatoes & Cucumber Salad

20 Min / 4 serving / Easy

Ingredients

- 2 cups (120g) sliced cucumber
- 2 cups (260g) cherry tomatoes, halved
- 1 tbsp fresh basil
- 1 tbsp chopped onion
- 2 tbsp extra virgin olive oil
- 2 tbsp vinegar
- 1 pinch oregano

In a bowl combine vegetables and herbs. Add olive oil and vinegar and stir until coated.

Serving size: 1 Total Fat: 2.5 g Saturated fat: 0.5 g Trans fat: 0 Calories: 55 Cholesterol: 0 Protein: 1.2 g Potassium: 254 mg Carbo: 6.9 g Fiber: 1.8 g Sugar: 3.5 g Sodium: 15.8 mg

Salmon Salad with Orange Vinaigrette

20 Min / 4 servings / Easy

Ingredients

- 5 oz (150g) fresh salmon fillets
- 2 oranges, zest
- 2 oranges, sliced
- 2 tbsp orange juice
- 2 tbsp balsamic vinegar
- 2 tbsp extra virgin olive oil
- 5 cups (375g) mixed salad greens
- 1 tbsp chopped white onion

Close salmon into baking paper and cook for 10-12 minutes in a covered non-sticking pan. Combine orange zest, juice, vinegar, and oil for the vinaigrette. In a bowl add greens, orange slices, and onion. Top with salmon fillets and vinaigrette.

Serving size: 1 total Fat: 5.4 g Saturated Fat: 1.3 g Trans Fat: 0 Calories: 100 Cholesterol: 22.5 mg

Protein: 9 g Potassium: 396 mg Carbo: 3.9 g Fiber: 1.5 g Sugar: 1.3 g Sodium: 36.9 mg

Green Salad with Beets and Edamame

15 min / 1 serving /Easy

Ingredients

- 1 cup (160g) shelled edamame
- 2 cups (100g) mixed salad greens
- 1/2 cup (70g) raw beet
- 2 tbsp red wine vinegar
- 1 tbs extra virgin olive oil
- Pepper to taste

Combine greens, edamame and beet in a bowl. Whisk vinegar, oil, and pepper. Drizzle over the salad.

Serving size: 1 Total Fat: 12.9 g Saturated Fat: 1 g Trans Fat: 0 Calories: 291 Cholesterol: 0 Protein: 18.1 g Potassium: 1257 mg Carbo: 25.5 g Fiber: 12 g Sugar: 4.5 g Sodium: 0

Red and Yellow Bell Peppers with Zucchini

40 Min / 3 servings / Easy

Ingredients

- 7 oz (200g) cubed zucchini
- 4 oz (115g) cubed yellow bell pepper
- 4 oz (115g) cubed red bell pepper
- 7 oz (200g) chopped potatoes
- 4 oz (115g) chopped white onions
- 2 tbsp extra virgin olive oil
- Pepper to taste

Put in a non-sticking pan oil, onion, red and yellow pepper, and potatoes and cook at medium heat for about 7-8 minutes. Add potatoes and cook all together for 10 minutes more. Vegetables must stay a little raw. Serve with meat.

Serving size: 1 Total Fat: 5.2 g Saturated Fat: 1 g Trans Fat: 0 Calories: 137 Cholesterol: 0 Protein: 4.3 g Potassium: 565 mg Carbo: 18 g Fiber: 0.7 g

Lemon Chickpeas Quinoa Salad

30 min / 3 servings / Easy

Ingredients
- *1/2 (110g) cup dry quinoa*
- *1/2 x 15 oz can (200g) low-sodium chickpeas, rinsed and well drained*
- *1/2 cup (60g) cucumber finely chopped*
- *1/2 cup (75g) red bell pepper, cubed*
- *1/2 cup (90g) cherry tomatoes, halved*
- *10 black olives*
- *1/2 cup (25g) white onion, chopped*
- *1 tbsp fresh dill*
- *1 lemon, juice and zest*
- *2 tbsp extra virgin olive oil*
- *Pepper to taste*

Boil water for quinoa and follow instructions. Make the dressing by mixing all ingredients in a bowl. Place all the vegetables in a large bowl, add quinoa, lemon juice and zest, pepper, olive oil.

Serving size: 1 Total Fat: 7.3 g Saturated Fat: 0.7 g Trans Fat: 0 Calories: 276 Cholesterol: 0 Protein: 10.3 g Potassium: 116 mg Carbo: 42 g Fiber: 7.5 g Sugar: 4.8 g Sodium: 190 mg

Sugar: 3 g Sodium. 17.5 mg

Eggplants & Tomatoes Skillet Italian-Style

1 hour / 4 servings / Easy / Microwave crisper

Ingredients

- 2 pounds (900g) eggplants
- 2 cups (350g) halved cherry tomatoes
- 1 tbsp fresh basil
- 4 tbsp extra virgin olive oil
- Pepper to taste

Wash eggplants with water, dry them well with a cloth, and dice them. Cook in the microwave crisper dish for 10-12 minutes (crisp function). Let them cool. In a non-sticking pan cook eggplants with 4 tbsp of oil for about 5-6 minutes or until light gold. Add tomatoes and cook for 10 minutes. Serve with basil on top.

Sering size: 1 Total Fat: 5.7 g Saturated Fat: 1 g Trans Fat: 0 Calories: 98 Cholesterol: 0 Protein: 3 g Potassium: 592 mg Carbo: 8.9 g Fiber: 1 g Sugar: 8.8 g Sodium: 72 mg

Summer Greens with Apple and Almonds

15 min / 4 servings / Easy

Ingredients

- 4 cups (300g) mixed salad greens
- 2 cups (350g) halved cherry tomato
- 1 big apple, chopped
- 1 big orange, chopped
- 1 cup (170g) boiled cannellini beans
- 1/2 cup (50g) almonds
- 1/2 cup (125g) fat free ricotta cheese
- 2 tbsp extra virgin olive oil
- 1 tbsp orange zest
- 2 tbsp orange juice

Put in a large bowl the greens, tomatoes, oranges, apples, almonds, cannellini beans, orange zest and ricotta. Mix oil, orange juice and zest apart and add to the salad.

Serving size: 1 Total Fat: 11.6 g Saturated Fat: 1.1 g Trans Fat: 0 Calories: 273 Cholesterol: 7.5 mg Protein: 11 g Potassium: 433 mg Carbo: 31.3 g Fiber: 6.5 g Sugar: 12.3 g Sodium: 65.1 mg

Sweet Potatoes Lentil Salad

1 hour / 4 servings / Easy

Ingredients

- 1 cup (200g) dry lentils
- 3 cups (750ml) water
- 2 cups (270g) diced sweet potatoes
- 1 tbsp onion, chopped
- 1 tsp basil
- 2 tbsp chopped fresh cilantro
- 1 garlic clove
- 1 tsp cumin
- 1 tbsp olive oil for lentils
- 1 tbsp olive oil for potatoes

Dressing

- 2 tbsp olive oil
- 2 tbsp balsamic vinegar
- 1 tbsp maple syrup
- 1 tbsp water

In a saucepan heat 1 tbsp olive oil over medium heat, add basil, cumin, and garlic and saute for about 1 minute. Add lentils and water and bring to a boil. The cooking time is about 15 minutes.

Roast sweet potato in oven to 425° F on baking paper with 1 tbsp of olive oil.

Once lentils are cooked drain off any excess water and pour into a serving bowl. Let them cool before adding all other ingredients.

Whisk together all ingredients of the vinaigrette and pour over the lentils.

Serving size: 1 Total Fat: 4.8 g Saturated Fat: 1 g Trans Fat: 0 Calories: 233 Cholesterol: 0 Protein: 9.4 g Potassium: 31.8 mg Carbo: 38 g Fiber: 10 g Sugar: 14 g Sodium: 14,8 mg

Healthy Sauteed Cabbage

30 min / 6 servings / Easy / Wok

Ingredients

- 2 pounds (900g) cabbage, thinly sliced
- 2 tbsp extra virgin olive oil
- 1 onion, sliced
- 2 garlic cloves, minced
- 2 tbsp shredded Parmesan cheese

Chop cabbage into slices. Saute garlic cloves and oil in a large skillet over medium-high heat for 2 minutes. Add cabbage and saute for 20-25 minutes. During this time, stir the cabbage occasionally until it becomes soft and caramelized.

Transfer to a large bowl and top with parmesan cheese.

Serving size: 1 Total Fat: 2.9 g Saturated Fat: 0.8 g Trans Fat: 0 Calories: 82 Cholesterol: 1.3 mg Protein: 3.8 g Potassium: 5.7 mg Carbo. 10 g Fiber: 0.2 g Sugar: 0.3 g Sodium: 29 mg

Sweet Potatoes and Kale Salad

50 min / 4 servings / Easy

Ingredients

- 1 tbsp olive oil
- 3 tbsp pumpkin seeds
- 2 cups (270g) cubed sweet potatoes
- 2 bunches of kale
- 1 apple, sliced thin
- 1/4 (32g) cup dried cranberries

Dressing

- 1/2 cup (120g) 0% fat free greek yogurt
- 3 tbsp vinegar
- 1 tbs maple syrup
- 6 tbsp cold water

Preheat oven to 400° F.

Line a sheet pan with baking paper and place potatoes on it. Drizzle olive oil over them and toss together with your hands. Bake for 20-25 minutes. While the potatoes roast, combine all of the ingredients for the dressing. Add chopped kale to a serving bowl, then add potatoes, sliced apple, pumpkin seeds, and cranberries. Serve the salad with the dressing drizzled on top.

Serving size: 1 total Fat: 4.9 g Saturated Fat: 1 g Trans Fat: 0 Calories: 209 Cholesterol: 0 Protein: 6.9 g Potassium: 303 mg Carbo: 34.3 g Fiber: 4.3 g Sugar: 18.6 g Sodium: 47 mg

Beetroot Cutlets

40 min / 10 cutlets / Medium / Oven or Air Fryer

Ingredients

- 1 cup (150g) beetroot, boiled grated
- 1 cup (250g) potatoes, mashed
- 1/2 cup (110g) carrots, boiled and mashed
- 1/2 cup (80g) peas, boiled
- 1 whole green chili pepper
- 1 tsp cumin powder
- 1.5 tsp garam masala powder
- 1/2 tsp chilli powder
- 5 tbsp bread crumbs
- 3 tbsp oil

Mix in a bowl the grated beetroot, mashed potatoes and carrots, peas, chili, cumin, and garam masala powder. Divide dough into 10 equal portions and roll between both hands to form a log shape, slightly press to flatten. Put bread crumbs on a plate and dip cutlets to coat all sides. Cover an oven dish with a baking paper sheet, add oil and place cutlets. Bake at 400° F for 10-15 min turning to the other side.

Serving size: 1 cutlet Total Fat: 1.8 g Saturated Fat: 0.3 g Trans Fat: 0 Calories: 63 Cholesterol: 0.4 mg Protein: 1.3 g Potassium: 132 mg Carbo: 10 Fibeer: 1.9 g Sugar: 2.3 g Sodium: 156 mg

Southwestern Beans Salad

20 min / 6 servings / Easy

Ingredients

- 2 tomatoes, seeded and diced
- 15 oz (400g) can low sodium black beans
- 15 oz can (400g) low sodium kidney beans
- 3/4 cup (120g) corn, boiled
- 1 tbsp chopped cilantro
- 1 white onion, sliced
- 1 jalapeño diced
- 3 tbsp pumpkin seeds
- 1 little avocado, diced
- 1 lime juice
- 2 tbsp olive oil
- 1 tbsp maple syrup

Add beans, tomatoes, onion, jalapeño and pumpkin seeds to a large bowl. Combine in a glass the lime juice, syrup and olive oil for vinaigrette. Add tomatoes and onion, all diced avocado and fold in gently the salad. Season and serve it.

Serving size: 1 Total Fat: 9.9 g Saturated Fat: 1.5 g Trans Fat: 0 Calories: 266 Cholesterol: 0 Protein: 13 g Potassium: 318 mg Carbo: 31.8 g Fiber: 10 g Sugar: 4.6 g Sodium: 128 mg

Glazed Carrost and Sweet Potatoes Salad

50 min / 6 servings / Easy / Oven

Ingredients

- 1 pound (450g) sweet potatoes
- 2 pounds (900g) carrots
- 1/4 cup (80g) honey
- 1 garlic clove minced
- 2 tbsp extra virgin olive oil
- 1 tsp cinnamon
- 1 tsp ground ginger
- Pepper to taste
- 1 tbsp fresh parsley

Preheat oven to 425° F. Cut sweet potatoes and carrots the same size and toss them with all other ingredients, except parsley, in a large bowl. Roast for 40- 50 minutes in the oven, tossing once. Transfer to a serving dish and garnish with chopped parsley.

Serving size: 1 Total Fat: 2.2 g Saturated Fat: 0.3 g Trans Fat: 0 Calories: 170 Cholesterol: 0 Protein: 2.5 g Potassium: 553 mg Carbo: 35 g Fiber: 7.4 g Sugar: 24 g Sodium: 103 mg

Baked Zucchini and Potatoes Sticks

40 min / 2 servings / Easy / Oven

Ingredients
- 2 cups raw potatoes (300g)
- 2 cups zucchini sticks (300g)
- 1/2 tsp garlic powder
- 1 tsp onion powder
- 2 tsp smoked paprika
- 1 tbsp bread crumbs

Preheat the oven to 425° F. Cut zucchini and potatoes lengthwise into sticks. In a small bowl, mix together garlic powder, onion powder, bread crumbs and paprika. Sprinkle the seasoning on top of the sticks, tossing to coat them all evenly and spread them on a baking paper sheet. Bake for 30 minutes.

Serving size: 1 Total Fat: 1.8 g Saturated Fat: 0 Trans Fat: 0 Calories: 193 Cholesterol: 0 Protein: 6.1 g Potassium: 1503 mg Carbo: 38.3 g Fiber: 4.5 g Sugar: 6 Sodium: 83.5 mg

Veggie Potato Gateau

1 hour / 4 servings / Easy / Oven

Ingredients
- 1 lb (450g) potatoes, mashed
- 8 oz (220gr) zucchini, chopped
- 12 oz (350g) eggplants, chopped
- 8 oz (220g) red bell pepper, chopped
- 2 tbsp finely chopped onion
- 1 egg
- 4 tbsp bread crumbs
- 2 tbsp grated parmesan cheese
- 2 tbsp extra virgin olive oil

Preheat oven to 350° F. While potatoes are boiling (20-25 minutes) add oil and onion in a big non-sticking pan and saute for 2 min. Add eggplants and let saute for 5 min, then add chopped pepper and zucchini and let cook for 10-12 minutes all ingredients. Let vegetables cool. In a big bowl add vegetables to mashed potatoes, add parmesan too and mix with a spoon. Take a non-sticking baking pan and cover the base with 2 tbsp of bread crumbs, add your vegetable mix with a spatula. Cover with 2 tablespoons of bread crumbs and bake for 30 minutes.

Serving size: 1 Total Fat: 9.9 g Saturated Fat: 2 g Trans Fat: 0 Calories: 247 Cholesterol: 49 mg Protein: 7 g Potassium: 811mg Carbo: 32.5 g Fiber: 3.2 g Sugar: 4 g Sodium: 197.5 mg

Tuscany Panzanella Salad

50 min / 4 servings / Easy

Ingredients
- 2 cups (380g) halved cherry tomatoes
- 1 and 1/2 cup (200g) peeled and chopped cucumber
- 2 cups (260g) stale whole wheat bread
- 1/2 cup (60g) chopped onion
- 1 cup (250ml) water
- 3 tbsp extra virgin olive oil
- 1 tbsp white vinegar
- 2-3 fresh basil leaves

Chop stale bread into pieces, put them into a bowl, and cover with water. Let the bread soak up all water (about 20 minutes) then squeeze out all excess liquid and put all pieces in a large dish. Add halved cherry tomatoes, chopped onion, cucumber and basil leaves. Season with vinegar and oil.

Serving size: 1 Total Fat: 11.6 g Saturated Fat: 1.5 g Trans Fat: 0 Calories: 278 Cholesterol: 0 Protein: 6 g Potassium: 207.5 mg Carbo: 37.6 g Fiber: 6.3 g Sugar: 3.6 g Sodium: 15.4 mg

Low-Sodium Low-Fat Meat

Healthy Veggie Family Meatloaf

1 hour / 4 servings / Easy / Oven

Ingredients

- 1 pound (450g) extra-lean (95%) ground beef
- 6 tbsp oat bran
- 1/2 cup (120g) 0% fat greek yogurt
- 2 egg whites
- 1/2 cup (85g) shredded carrots
- 1/2 cup (55g) shredded zucchini
- 2 tbsp chopped onion
- 2 tbsp extra virgin olive oil

Preheat the oven to 400° F. Heat olive oil in a skillet on medium heat, cook and stir onion, zucchini and carrots for 5 to 10 minutes. In a large bowl combine meat and cool vegetables, oat bran, greek yogurt and egg whites, mix well using your hands. Press the meat mixture into a loaf pan and bake for 35-40 minutes.

Serving size: 1 Total Fat: 19.8 g Saturated Fat: 5.5 g Trans Fat: 0 Calories: 373 Cholesterol: 74.4 mg Protein: 31.4 g Potassium: 395 mg Carbo: 17.2 g Fiber: 3.6 g Sugar: 2.2 g Sodium: 127.3 mg

Baked Turkey Meatballs

40 mins / 4 servings / Easy / Oven

Ingredients
- 1 pound (450 g) ground turkey
- 1 cup (80 g) rolled oats
- 1/2 cup (120 g) 0% fat greek yogurt
- 2 egg whites
- 1 tbsp onion, chopped
- 1 garlic clove, chopped

Preheat oven to 400°F. Line a baking pan with parcel paper. Add in a bowl all ingredients and mix them well. With both hands take some meat mix and roll 2-inch balls. Place all your meatballs on the baking pan and bake for 20-22 minutes.

Serving size: 1 Total Fat: 12.6 g Saturated Fat: 3.4 g Trans Fat: 0 Calories: 285 Cholesterol: 85.6 mg Protein: 27.9 g Potassium: 102 mg Carbo: 15 Fiber: 2 g Sugar: 1.3 g Sodium: 129 mg

Easy Baked Boneless Chicken Thighs

2 hours / 3 servings / Easy Oven

Ingredients
- 3 boneless, skinless chicken thighs
- 1 garlic clove, chopped
- 1 tbsp fresh parsley, chopped
- 2 tbsp. extra-virgin olive oil
- 6 tbsp water
- 6 tbsp balsamic vinegar
- 1 tbsp maple syrup
- 2 tbsp mustard
- 1 pinch of pepper

IIn a bowl mix all ingredients, except chicken and whisk with a fork. Add chicken and let marinate for up to 1 hour, better two. Preheat oven to 400° F. Place chicken in a baking pan and cover with leftover marinade. Bake for 20 minutes or until golden.

Serving size: 1 Total Fat: 15.3 g Saturated Fat: 3.3 g Trans Fat: o Calories: 266 Cholesterol: 75 mg Protein: 16 g Potassium: 60 mg Carbo: 16 g Fiber: 0.7 g Sugar: 12.3 g Sodium: 70.7 mg

Orange Chicken Cutlets

40 mins / 4 servings / Easy / Oven

Ingredients
- 1.3 pounds (600g) boneless, skinless chicken brest sliced
- 1 egg + 2 egg whites
- 1/2 cup (65g) whole wheat bread crumbs
- 1 tsp ground paprika

Sauce
- 1 tbsp maple syrup
- 1 orange, zest and juice
- 1 tsp curry powder

Preheat the oven to 400° F. Beat egg and egg whites in a bowl. Place bread crumbs on a plate. Lay chicken slice opened on a serving plate and sprinkle with paprika. Dip slices in eggs and then in bread crumbs on each side of them. Lay slices on a non-sticking baking pan and bake for 16-20 minutes, turning halfway through. In a glass mix orange, juice and zest, syrup and curry, microwave for a few seconds and drizzle on chicken for 5 minutes before turning off the oven.

Serving size: 1 Total Fat: 6 g Saturated Fat: 2 g Trans Fat: 0 Calories: 262 Cholesterol: 142,5 mg Protein: 37 g Potassium: 677 mg Carbo: 15 g Fiber: 2.1 g Sugar: 6.4 g Sodium: 307.8 mg

Healthy Pepper Chicken Fajitas

50 mins / 4 servings / Easy / Oven

Ingredients
- 1 lb (450g) chicken breasts sliced thinly
- 8 oz (225g) red bell pepper sliced
- 8 oz (225g) yellow pepper sliced
- 1 onion, sliced
- 1 orange, juice

- 2 tbsp extra virgin olive oil
- 2 tbsp. Taco seasonings spices mix (seasoning Chapter)

Preheat oven to 400° F. Line a baking sheet with parchment paper. In a bowl add sliced chicken, pepper and onion and spread with the orange juice and toss well. Add taco seasoning spices and toss again. Spread chicken and vegetables on the baking sheet and bake for 30-35 minutes.

Serving size: 1 Total Fat: 8.7 g Saturated Fat: 1 g Trans Fat: 0 Calories: 224 Cholesterol: 0 Protein: 21.4 g Potassium: 43.5 mg Carbo: 15.1 g Fiber: 0.5 g Sugar: 3.8 g Sodium: 7.5 mg

Creamy Tofu and Turkey Salad

20 mins / 2 servings / Super Easy

Ingredients

- 10 oz (280g) cooked turkey breast, diced
- 1/2 (50g) cup celery, diced
- 2 tbsp fresh cilantro, chopped
- 1 red onion, chopped
- 1 cup (180g) cherry tomatoes, halved
- 5 oz (110g) hard tofu, diced

Dressing

- 2 tbsp olive oil
- 2 tsp mustard
- 1 tbsp lemon juice
- 1 garlic clove, chopped
- Pepper to taste

In a large bowl mix turkey, tofu, tomatoes, celery, cilantro, and onion. In a glass mix all the dressing ingredients with a teaspoon and pour in the salad bowl. Whisk well with a wooden spoon.

Serving size: 1 Total Fat: 17.6 g Saturated Fat: 3.9 g Trans Fat: 0 Calories: 373 Cholesterol: 70 mg Protein: 40.4 g Potassium: 893 mg Carbo: 13.3 g Fiber: 2 g Sugar: 10 g Sodium: 114.6 mg

Sweet Potato & Peas Lamb Chops

50 mins / 3 servings / Easy / Oven

Ingredients

- 3 rib lamb chops (5 oz-140g each)
- 14 oz (400g) sweet potatoes diced
- 1 cup (150g) frozen peas, boiled
- 3 tbsp olive oil
- 1 onion chopped
- 1 tbsp of steak seasoning mix (Seasoning Chapter)

Preheat oven to 350° F. Put in a non-sticking baking pan potatoes, peas, onion and lamb chops. Spread with seasoning all over and the olive oil. Bake for 40-50 minutes or until ready.

Serving size: 1 Total Fat: 33.8 g Satureted Fat: 2 g Trans Fat: 0 Calories: 574 Cholesterol: 0 Protein: 32 g Potassium: 704 mg Carbo: 35.4 g Fiber: 6.3 g Sugar: 12.7 g Sodium: 102 mg

Homemade Ground Turkey Burgers

1 hour / 4 servings / Easy

Ingredients

- 4 whole wheat hamburger buns (1.75 oz -50g each)
- 1 1/4 pound (560g) ground turkey
- 1 1/2 cups (45g) fresh spinach, chopped
- 1 garlic clove, minced
- 1/4 cup (40g) italian bread crumbs
- 2 tsp low sodium Worcestershire sauce
- 1 tbsp extra virgin olive oil
- 1 cucumber, sliced
- 4 red onion slices

Mix in a bowl the ground turkey, chopped spinach, chopped garlic, bread crumbs, Worcestershire, and olive oil until combined. Divide into 4 equal portions. Oil the grates of a grill and preheat to medium-high. Grill burgers for about 4-5 minutes per side. Serve on buns with cucumber and red onion.

Serving size: 1 Total Fat: 16.3 g Saturated Fat: 1.4 g Trans Fat: 0 Calories: 424 Cholesterol: 96.6 mg Protein: 32.8 g Potassium: 469 mg Carbo: 36.7 g Fiber: 2.6 g Sugar: 3 g Sodium: 283 mg

Easy Grilled Pineapple Chicken

30 mins / 2 servings / Easy /

Ingredients

- 12 oz (350g) boneless, skinless chicken breast

Marinade

- 1/4cup natural 100% pineapple juice
- 1 tbsp granulated erythritol
- 3 tbsp extra virgin olive oil
- 2 tbsp similar ketchup (4 tbsp tomato sauce + 1 tsp vinegar + 1 tsp granulated erythritol)
- 1 garlic clove minced
- 1/2 tsp chili powder
- 1 pinch ground pepper

Whisk in a bowl oil, pineapple juice, erythritol, similar ketchup, garlic, chili powder, and pepper. Cover chicken with marinade and refrigerate for 30 -60 minutes up to 24 hours. Heat the grill on medium-high heat, place chicken breast, and cook for 4-5 minutes per side. Brush chicken with marinade several times, until it is ready.

Serving size: 1 Total Fat: 22.8 g Saturated Fat: 3 g Trans Fat: 0 Calories: 364 Cholesterol: 0 Protein: 29.9 g Potassium: 6 mg Carbo: 9.8 g Fiber: 0 Sugar: 0 Sodium: 13 mg

Mediterranean Grilled Chicken

30 mins / 2 servings / Easy / Grill

Ingredients

- 1 lb (450 g) boneless chicken breast

Marinade

- 2 tbsp (30g) olive oil
- 2 tbsp of balsamic vinegar
- 3 tbsp of water
- 1 tbsp orange or lemon juice
- 1 tsp all spice
- 1 tsp oregan
- 1 tsp parsley
- 1 tsp rosemary
- 1 pinch of black pepper

Combine all the marinade ingredients, toss the chicken and set aside. Preheat the grill to medium heat. Place chicken on the grill and cook for 5-6 minutes per side. Use marinade to wet it.

Serving size: 1 Total Fat: 22.1 g Saturated Fat: 6 g Trans Fat: 0 Calories: 415 Cholesterol: 130 mg Protein: 50.5 g Potassium: 43.5 mg Carbo: 3.5 g Fiber: 0 Sugar: 2 g Sodium: 85.4 mg

Italian Marinara Meatballs

40 mins / 20 meatballs / Easy / Oven
- 1 lb (450g) ground beef
- 10 oz (280g) ground turkey
- 1/2 cup (112g) 0% fat greek yogurt
- 8 tbsp oat bran
- 1 egg white
- 1 tsp fresh parsley chopped

Marinara Sauce
- 2 x 15 oz can (800g) diced tomatoes
- 1 tbsp extra virgin olive oil
- 1 tsp oregan
- 1 garlic clove, chopped
- 1 tsp fresh parsley chopped

Preheat oven to 350° F and line a large sheet with parchment paper. Combine all ingredients in a bowl and mix. Divide into 20 and form balls with both hands. Place balls on a baking sheet and bake for about 20 minutes. Heat a saucepan to medium heat, add olive oil, garlic, diced tomatoes, oregano and parsley and simmer for 8-10 minutes. Add meatballs carefully and simmer for 8-10 minutes.

Serving size: 1 meatball Total Fat: 4.8 g Saturated Fat: 1.4 g Trans Fat: 0 Calories:104 Cholesterol: 25.4 mg Protein: 9.3 g Carbo: 5.8 g Fiber: 0.8 g Sugar: 1.7 g Sodium: 46.1 mg

Easy Mexican Taco Turkey Meatloaf

1 hour 30 / 3 servings / Easy
- 1 lbs (450g) ground turkey
- 1 egg white
- 2 tbsp oat bran
- 8 oz (200g) diced peeled tomatoes
- 1 tbsp olive oil
- 2 tbsp of Taco seasoning spices mix (Seasoning Chapter)

Preheat oven to 450° F. Blend diced tomatoes to high speed few seconds, just to have a smooth salsa. Grease a loaf pan with olive oil. Add in a bowl ground turkey, half of salsa, oat bran and spices. Mix ingredients untill well incorporated. Give it the form you like in the loaf pan and pour the rest of the salsa over the top of the meatloaf. Bake for 45-60 minutes.

Serving size: 1 Total Fat: 20.4 g Saturated Fat: 5.2 g Trans Fat: 0 Calories: 344 Cholesterol: 112.5 mg Protein: 30.7 g Potassium: 17.7 mg Carbo: 9.4 g Fiber: 1.3 g Sugar: 2.5 g Sodium: 163.3 mg

Yummy Creamy Spinach Turkey Skillet

35 mins / 3 servings / Medium / Oven-safe Skillet
- 1 lb (450g) turkey breast, divided in 4
- 1 tbsp olive oil
- 1 garlic clove, chopped
- 1 tsp fresh parsley, chopped
- 1 cup (225g) 0% fat greek yogurt
- 2 cups (480ml) skimmed milk
- 3 cups (100g) spinach, chopped
- 1 pound (450g) yellow bell peppers
- 3 cups (480g) cauliflower
- 1 tbsp fresh parsley, chopped

Preheat oven to 350° F. In a large oven-safe skillet saute oil, parsley and garlic for 2 minutes, add turkey and cook for about 2 minutes on each side, no more. While the turkey is cooking, cut the cauliflower into chunks, place it into a food processor and pulse until resembles the texture of rice. Set aside. Cut bell peppers into strips and set aside. Blend yogurt, milk and spinach. Add cauliflower and pepper to the oven-safe skillet, layer sauce on top and tan the chicken. Transfer to oven and bake for 20 minutes or until cauliflower and pepper are fully cooked.

Serving size: 1 Total Fat: 7.5 g Saturated Fat: 2.2 g Trans Fat: 0 Calories: 400 Cholesterol: 3.3 mg Protein: 55.2 g Potassium: 1246 mg Carbo: 27.8 g Fiber. 4.3 g Sugar: 19.5 g Sodium: 274 mg

Orange and Onion Chicken

20 mins / 3 servings / Easy/ Pan

- 3 skinless (1 lb-450g), boneless chicken breast halves - cut into strips
- 1/2 cup (60g) whole wheat flour
- 1 medium onion, sliced
- 2 orange, zest and juice
- 3 tbsp olive oil

Add chicken and flour to a seal bag and shake to coat. Set aside. Heat a pan to medium-high and add oil and onion, saute for 3-4 minutes. Add chicken strips, half of the orange juice and zest to the onion and saute for 10 to 15 minutes. When ready spread with the other part of orange juice and serve.

Serving size: Total Fat: 15.6 g Saturated Fat: 2 g Trans Fat: 0 Calories: 387 Cholesterol: 0 Protein: 37.9 g Potassium: 145 mg Carbo: 23.8 g Fiber: 6.3 g Sodium: 3.3 mg

Spinach & Chickpeas Lemon-spiced Chicken

20 mins / 3 servings / Easy / Saucepan
Ingredients

- 14 oz (400g) chicken breast chunks
- 1 x 15 can (400g) low sodium chickpeas
- 8 oz (220g) spinach, chopped
- 1 little onion, chopped
- 2 tbsp olive oil
- 1 lemon, zest and juice
- 2 cups (500ml) low sodium vegetables broth

Heat the oil in a large saucepan and saute onion for 2 minutes, add chicken chunks, lemon, zest and juice and saute until ready. Add chickpeas and broth, cover and simmer for 4-5 minutes. Add spinach, cover the pan and let simmer for 2-3 minutes more.

Serving size:1 Total Fat: 13.3 g Saturated Fat: 1.3 g Trans Fat: 0 Calories: 393 Cholesterol: 0 Protein: Potassium: 548 mg Carbo: 27.9 g Fiber: 3.3 g Sugar: 2.7 g Sodium: 199 mg

Pepper & Broccoli Chicken Pan

50 mins / 4 servings / Medium / Oven

- 14 oz (400g) chicken breast
- 1 cup (200g) white rice uncooked
- 3 cups (270g) broccoli, chopped
- 2 cups (300g) red bell pepper, diced
- 2 tbsp onion, chopped
- 2 tbsp olive oil
- 1 cup (225g) 0% fat greek yogurt
- 1 cup (240ml) skimmed milk (hot)
- 1 cup water

Cut broccoli, chicken and pepper into 1-inch pieces. Heat a large saucepan on medium-high, add oil and onion and saute for 2 minutes. Add pepper, rice, chicken, milk and water and toss to combine. Cover the saucepan and cook for 4-5 minutes stirring occasionally. Add broccoli and hot milk and continue simmering until rice is ready..

Serving size: 1 Total Fat: 8.3 g Saturated Fat: 1g Trans Fat: 0 Calories: 436 Cholesterol: 0 Protein: 35.6 g Potassium: 41.8 mg Carbo: 55 g Fiber: 2.9 g Sugar: 7.7 g Sodium: 34 mg

Low-Sodium Low-Fat Seafood

Easy Honey Garlic Salmon

20 mins / 2 servings / Easy / Pan

Ingredients

- 2 salmon fillet (6 oz-180g each)
- 1 tsp paprika
- 1 tbsp extra virgin olive oil
- 1 tbsp water
- 1 garlic clove, chopped
- 4 walnuts, chopped
- 3 tbsp balsamic vinegar
- 2 tbsp honey
- 1 orange, juice and zest
- Orange wedges to serve

Season salmon fillet with paprika on each side. Heat oil in a pan over medium heat, add garlic and saute for 1 minute. Add walnuts, honey, vinegar, orange zest, and juice, and allow the flavors to heat through and combine. Add salmon steaks to the sauce and cook for 6-7 minutes on each side. Add orange wedges around the salmon.

Serving size: 1 Total Fat: 30.8 g Saturated Fat: 2 g Trans Fat: 0 Calories: 491 Cholesterol: 5 mg Protein: 38.3 g Potassium: 162 mg Carbo: 15.3 g fiber: 1.5 g Sugar: 10.5 g Sodium: 28.5 mg

Lemon Baked Cod

30 mins / 2 servings / Easy / Oven

Ingredients

- 12 oz (350g) cod fillets
- 1 tbsp extra virgin olive oil
- 1 garlic clove, sliced
- 1 lemon, zest and juice
- 1 pinch of smoked paprika
- 1 tbsp fresh parsley, chopped

Preheat oven to 400° F.

In a glass add olive oil, lemon juice, chopped parsley and garlic and whisk well. Pour half of the mixture into a non-sticking baking pan, place cod fillets and sprinkle the remaining mix on top of the fish. Add 4-5 tbsp of water and sprinkle the paprika on top. Bake for 15 - 17 minutes. Garnish with lemon slices.

Serving size: 1 Total Fat: 12.5 g Saturated Fat: 1 g Trans Fat: 0 Calories: 160 Cholesterol: 17.5 mg Protein: 9.2 g Potassium: 66.5 mg Carbo: 2.8 g Fiber: 0.5 g Sugar: 0.5 g Sodium: 37.5 mg

Spiced Tilapia with Tomatoes

20 min / 2 servings / Easy / Skillet pan

Ingredients

- 12 oz (350g) tilapia fillets
- 1 cup (230g) chopped tomatoes
- 1 tbsp extra virgin olive oil
- 1 garlic clove
- 3-4 fresh basil leaves
- 1 tbsp fresh chopped parsley

Heat a skillet pan on medium heat, add oil and garlic and saute for 2 minutes. Add chopped tomatoes and basil, stir and cook for 4-5 minutes or until tomatoes are soft. Add fish fillets to the sauce, cover and cook for 3-4 minutes on each side. Serve with fresh chopped parsley on top.

Serving size: 1 Total Fat: 11.1 g Saturated Fat: 1 g Trans Fat: 0 Calories: 252 Cholesterol: 52.5 mg Protein: 33 g Potassium: 20 mg Carbo: 5.1 g Fiber: 0 Sugar: 0 Sodium: 91.5 mg

Parsley Lime Halibut Fillets

10 mins / 2 serving / Easy /Skillet pan

Ingredients

- 1 pound (450g) halibut fillets
- 1 tbsp extra virgin olive oil
- 2 tbsp fresh lime juice + zest of 1
- 1 tbsp fresh parsley, chopped
- 1 garlic clove

In a bowl coat halibut fillets with garlic, parsley and half of the lime juice. Heat a skillet pan on medium heat and add oil and fillets. Cook no more than 2 minutes on each side. Spread the remaining lime juice and the lime zest and serve immediately.

Serving size: 1 Total Fat: 14.9 g *Saturated Fat: 1 g* Trans Fat: 0 *Calories: 366 Cholesterol: 0* Protein: 53.5 g Potassium: 54 mg Carbo: 4.4 g Fiber: 1 g Sugar: 0 *Sodium: 1.5 mg*

Pepper Crusted Ahi Tuna & Arugula Salad

20 min / 2 servings / Easy / Skillet pan

Ingredients

- 2 ahi tuna steaks (8 oz-230g)
- 1/2 tsp ground black pepper
- 1 tbsp olive oil
- 3 tbsp black sesame seeds

Dressing

- 4 tbsp fresh lime juice
- 1 tbsp maple syrup
- 1 tbsp extra virgin olive oil
- 1 tbsp sesame oil
- 2 tbsp grated ginger

Salad

- 5 cups (100g) packed aragula
- 1/2 apple, thinly sliced
- 1 radish, thinly sliced

Season tuna with pepper on both sides. Pour black sesame seeds on a large plate and press tuna steak into the seeds to coat them on all sides. Heat a skillet pan on medium-high heat with oil, add tuna and cook 30 seconds to 1 minute per side. In a glass mix all the dressing ingredients. Slice tuna. In a large bowl combine aragula, apple and radish with dressing, then transfer to a large serving plate, add tuna on top.

Serving size: 1 Total Fat: 29 g *Saturated Fat: 4.5 g* Trans Fat: 0 *Calories: 480 Cholesterol: 50.7 mg* Protein: 31 g Potassium: 158 mg Carbo: 22.7 g Fiber: 3.4 g Sugar: 13.2 g *Sodium: 67.7 mg*

Broiled Garlic Tilapia & Grenn Beans

20 mins / 2 servings / Easy / Broiler

Ingredients

- 2 tilapia fillets (6 oz-170g) each
- 2 tbsp olive oil
- 1 garlic clove, chopped

- 1 tsp oregano
- 2 tbsp fresh parsley
- 1 lemon, zest and juice of 1 half
- 2 cups (200g) green beans

Boil green beans in hot water until tender. Line the broiler pan with foil. Adjust the top rack 6 to 8 inches from the heating element. Place fillets on the foil and season with 1 tbsp of oil, oregano, parsley and garlic. Set broiler to low and place fish on the rack. Cook until fish flakes easily with a fork, about 6 to 8 minutes. You don't need to turn the fish. In a bowl season green beans with the other olive oil tablespoon and lemon. Pour green beans into a plate and top with fish fillets.

Serving size: 1 Total Fat: 17.9 g Saturated Fat: 2 g Trans Fat: 0 Calories: 333 Cholesterol: 52.5 mg Protein: 33.6 g Potassium: 260 mg Carbo: 9.3 g Fiber: 3 g Sugar: 0.5 g Sodium: 98.5 mg

Flounder Fillets & Black Olive Tomato Sauce

20 mins / 2 servings / Easy / Skillet

Ingredients
- 2 flounder fillets 6 oz (170g) each
- 1 tbsp extra virgin olive oil
- 1 garlic clove, chopped
- 1 cup (150g) chopped cherry tomatoes
- 1 tbsp white onion, chopped
- 1/4 cup (45g) pitted black olives
- 3-4 tbsp of water
- 1 tbsp fresh chopped parsley

Heat oil in a skillet pan to medium heat. Add garlic and saute for 1-2 minutes. Add chopped cherry tomatoes, onion, water and black olives and saute for 3-4 minutes, until tomatoes become soft. Add fillets to the sauce and let them cook for 2-3 minutes each side. Serve immediately with a spoon or two of sauce as topping.

Serving size: 1 Total Fat: 13.2 g Saturated Fat: 1.5 g Trans Fat: 0 Calories: 302 Cholesterol: 114 mg Protein: 41.7 g Potassium: 769 mg Carbo: 4.1 g Fiber: 1.9 g Sugar: 2.8 g Sodium: 179.3 mg

Blackened Cod & Tomato Basil Salade

30 mins / 2 servings / Easy / Skillet

Ingredients

- 2 cod fillets 6 oz (170g) each
- 1 tbsp sweet paprika
- 1 tbsp chili powder
- 1/2 tbsp ground cummin
- 1/2 tsp black pepper
- 1 pinch cayenne pepper
- 2 tbsp olive oil

Salad

- 2 cups (300g) halved cherry tomatoes
- 1 tbsp extra virgin olive oil
- 1 tbsp fresh basil, chopped
- 1 celery stick, sliced

Combine in a bowl all spices, then pour them into a large plate. Add fish fillets to the mix and press well on each side. Heat, in a skillet pan to medium heat, oil, add spiced fillets and cook for 5 - 7 minutes each side, until the fish flakes easily with a fork. In a bowl whisk olive oil, basil, celery and tomatoes. When the fillets are cooked serve with tomato salad.

Serving size: 1 Total Fat: 27.2 g Saturated Fat: 3 g Trans Fat: 0 Calories: 338 Cholesterol: 17 mg Protein: 10.6 g Potassium: 367 mg Carbo: 12.7 g Fiber: 7.3 g Sugar: 4.5 g Sodium: 56 mg

Florentine Sea Bass & Creamy Spinach

20 mins / 2 servings / Easy / Skillet

Ingredients

- 2 sea bass fillet 6 oz (170g) each
- 1 cup (150g) red bell pepper chopped
- 5 oz (150g) fresh baby spinach
- 3 oz (90g) low fat ricotta cheese
- 2 tbsp skimmed milk
- 1 garlic clove
- 2 tbsp olive oil

Heat a large skillet pan to medium-high heat, add 1 tbsp of oil and garlic clove chopped and saute for 2 minutes. Add peppers and continue cooking for about 4 minutes. Add spinach and mix until the spinach wilts down. Mix in a bowl ricotta cheese and skimmed milk, then add to the skillet pan, toss well and turn the heat off. Heat another skillet pan to medium heat, with the other tablespoon of oil, add the fish and cook for 3-4 minutes on each side. Divide the spinach mixture on the bottom of each plate and top with fillets.

Serving size: 1 Total Fat: 27.3 g Saturated Fat: 6 g Trans Fat: 0 Calories: 450 Cholesterol: 11.3 mg Protein: 41.4 g Potassium: 6 mg Carbo: 9.7 g Fiber: 1.5 g Sugar: 5.3 g Sodium: 100 mg

Tuna & Avocado Salad

30 mins / 2 servings / Easy / Skillet pan

Ingredients

- 12 oz (340g) fresh tuna
- 1 avocado (4oz-1200g) cubed
- 1 cups (150g) halved cherry tomatoes
- 1/2 cucumber (6oz -150g) sliced
- 2 tbs olive oil
- 1 tsp fresh basil chopped
- 1 garlic clove, chopped
- 1 tbs balsamic vinegar

Combine in a bowl halved tomatoes, cucumber slices, and diced avocado, In a glass mix 1 tbsp of olive oil, garlic, basil and balsamic vinegar, whisk well with a fork. Add dressing into salad and toss. Heat a skillet pan to medium-high heat, add 1 tbsp of oil and tuna and cook 2 minutes each side. When fillets are ready put them on top of your salad and serve.

Serving size: 1 Total Fat: 30.6 g Saturated Fat: 5.3 g Trans Fat: 0 Calories: 488 Cholesterol: 74 mg Protein: 42.3 g Potassium: 411 mg Carbo: 11 g Fiber: 5.7 g Sugar: 4.2 g Sodium: 70.2 mg

Grilled Snapper in Orange Sauce

1 hour / 4 servings / Medium / Broiler
Ingredients
- 1 fresh snapper (2.2lb-1kg)
- 2 tbsp extra virgin olive oil
- 1 tbsp fresh parsley, chopped

Sauce
- 1 cup (235g) fresh orange juice
- 2 tsp orange zest
- 2 tbsp cornstarch
- 1/2 cup (125ml) water
- 2 tbsp maple syrup
- 2 tbsp balsamic vinegar
- 1/2 lime juice
- 4 orange slices to garnish

Adjust the top rack 6 to 8 inches from the heating element. Wipe out the fish cavity and brush the skin with oil. Set broiler to medium-high and place fish on the rack. Cook until fish flakes easily with a fork, about 6 to 8 minutes on each side. Combine cornstarch with water and bring to a boil. Set aside. In a little saucepan, over medium heat, combine cornstarch cream with orange juice, zest, syrup, vinegar and lime. Heat and simmer for 4-5 minutes. Transfer snapper to a serving plate, spread with parsley and cover with orange sauce. Serve immediately.

Serving size: 1 Total Fat: 10.3 g Saturated Fat: 1.5 g Trans Fat: 0 Calories: 407 Cholesterol: 92.5 mg Protein: 51.9 g Potassium: 1162.5 mg Carbo: 26.7 g Fiber: 0 Sugar: 11.8 g Sodium: 162.1 mg

Baked Tilapia with Garlic and Herbs

30 mins / 2 servings / Easy / Oven
Ingredients
- 2 tilapia fillets (6 oz-170g)
- 2 tbsp olive oil
- 3 tbsp water
- 2 tbsp fresh parsley chopped
- 3 tbsp whole wheat bread crumbs
- 3 tbsp sesame seeds
- 1 pinch of ground pepper
- 1/2 garlic clove chopped
- 1/2 tsp aniseed

Preheat the oven to 400° F. Grease a baking pan with non-sticking spray and place the fillets. Heat a little saucepan on medium heat, add oil and water, bring to a boil and turn off. Brush both sides of the fish with oil and water mix. Add in water and oil bread crumbs, sesame, pepper, garlic, parsley and aniseed and mix well. Spread and press the bread crumbs mixture over the fillets. Bake in the preheated oven for 12 minutes.

Serving size: Total Fat: 7.4 g Saturated Fat: 0.2 g Trans Fat: 0 Calories: 258 Cholesterol: 52.5 mg Protein: 34.9 g Potassium: 21 mg Carbo: 13 g Fiber: 2.5 g Sugar: 1.8 g Sodium: 231.4 mg

Crispy Lemon Sea Bass

30 mins / 2 servings / Easy / Skillet
Ingredients
- 12 oz (350g) sea bass fillets
- 2 tbsp olive oil
- 2 egg whites
- 1 &1/2 cup (40g) whole wheat corn flakes
- 1 tbsp white vinegar + 2 tbsp water
- 1/3 cup (80ml) fresh lemon juice

Whisk the egg whites in a dish. Pour bread crumbs into another dish. Dip fillets into egg whites, then into bread crumbs, pressing lightly. Heat olive oil over medium heat in a pan and saute fillets until golden, about 3 minutes on each side. In a small saucepan, heat the lemon juice, water and vinegar over medium-low heat until the mixture is reduced by half. Drizzle sauce lightly over the crispy fillets.

Serving size: 1 Total Fat: 24.3 g Saturated Fat: 3.8 g Trans Fat: 0 Calories: 495 Cholesterol: 0 Protein: 42.8 g Potassium: 133 mg Carbo: 26.4 g Fiber:4 g Sugar: 5 g Sodium: 83 mg

Sheet Pan Teriyaki Salmon

30 mins / 2 servings / Easy Oven
Ingredients
- 2 (8oz-230g) salmon fillets
- 1 cup (70g) broccoli florets
- 1 cup diced yellow bell pepper
- 1 cup (150g) diced red bell pepper
- 2 cups (150g) broccoli florets
- 7 oz (110g) sweet potatoes diced
- 1 carrot, sliced
- 4 tbsp balsamic vinegar
- 1 tbsp maple syrup
- 1 tbsp each: paprika, garlic, oregan
- 1/2 tsp ground ginger
- 1 tbsp cornstarch
- 1 tbsp sesame seeds

Grease a sheet pan with a non-sticking spray and lay on all the vegetables and salmon fillets. Preheat the oven to 400° F. In a bowl combine vinegar, syrup, garlic, oregan, paprika, ginger and cornstarch. Drizzle all the sauce on vegetables and salmon. Bake for 20-25 minutes. When fish and vegetables are ready spread sesame seed on top.

Serving size: 1 Total Fat: 18.4 g Saturated Fat: 0 Trans Fat: 0 Calories: 461 Cholesterol: 69 mg Protein: 31.3 g Potassium: 771 mg Carbo: 42.6 g Fiber: 7.4 g Sugar: 17.5 g Sodium: 134.8 mg

Grilled Tandoori Catfish

30 mins / 2 servings / Easy / Oven
Ingredients

- 1 lb (450g) catfish fillets (cod, tilapia, halibut work well too)
- 1 tsp for each: ginger, turmeric, dry coriander powder, tandoori masala, chili powder, dry grated garlic, cumin
- 1 tbsp oregan
- 1 tbsp olive oil
- 1 tbs balsamic vinegar

Combine all ingredients in a bowl and toss the fillets well. Set aside for 30 minutes. Heat oven to 400° F. Line the bottom of the crisper pan with parchment paper and lay down fillets. Bake for 12-15 minutes. Time will vary based on the thickness of the fish.

Serving size: 1 Total Fat: 28 g Saturated Fat: 1 g Trans Fat: 0 Calories: 413 Cholesterol: 0 Protein: 35.7 g Potassium: 69 mg Carbo: 4.6 g Fiber: 1.5 g Sugar: 1 g Sodium: 68 mg

Anchovies Marinated in Vinegar

20 mins + 2 hours / 2 servings / Easy /
Ingredients
- 1 pound (450g) fresh anchovies
- 1 cup (250ml) white vinegar
- 1 tsp oregan
- 2 garlic cloves, chopped
- 2 tbsp extra virgin olive oil
- 1/2 tsp hot chili pepper

Clean the anchovies, removing heads and spines, then removing innards with your fingers. Rinse them well under water and lay them flat on an upside-down glass to dry. Cover with white vinegar for 1,30-2 hours or until they whiten. Drain vinegar, place anchovies in one serving plate, and spread oregano, garlic, hot chili pepper, and extra virgin olive oil. Serve after 30 minutes.

Serving size: 1 Total Fat: 6.8 g Saturated Fat: 0.2 g Trans Fat: 0 Calories: 229 Cholesterol: 157 mg Protein: 37.9 g Potassium: 6 mg Carbo: 3.9 g Fiber: 0 Sugar: 0 Sodium: 0.5 mg

Low-Sodium Low-Fat Savory Pies & Pizza

Spanakopita: a Greek Savory Pie

2 hours / 6 servings / Medium / Oven

Ingredients
- 1 pound (450g) fresh spinach
- 2 sheet - Homemade Olive Oil Phyllo sheet (Doughs chapter)
- 1/2 cup (125g) fat-free ricotta cheese
- 1/2 cup (125g) 0% fat greek yogurt
- 1 egg + 2 egg whites
- 1/4 cup (40g) crumbled, fat-free feta
- pepper

Preheat oven to 350° F. Lightly spray an 8- or 9-inch square baking dish with cooking spray. Boil spinach for 3-4 minutes, then chop them with a fork and knife. In a bowl mix ricotta, yogurt, eggs, crumbled feta and pepper, add chopped spinach. Place 1 phyllo sheet into the baking dish, transfer the spinach mixture to the baking dish too and cover with another phyllo sheet. Bake for 45-50 minutes.

Serving size: 1 (filling + phyllo sheets) Total Fat: 12.2 g Saturated Fat: 2.4 g Trans Fat: 0 Calories: 550 Cholesterol: 41.8 mg Protein: 26,7 g Potassium: 548.8 mg Carbo: 79.9 g Fiber: 3.7 g Sugar: 4.7 g Sodium: 227.4 mg

Fresh Zucchini Pie

1 hour / 8 servings / Easy / Oven

Ingredients
- 4 cups (500g) sliced fresh zucchini
- 1 Homemade Olive Oil Phyllo dough 1 sheet (Doughs chapter)
- 2 tbsp olive oil
- 1/2 fresh chopped onion
- 1/2 cup (125g)fat-free ricotta cheese
- 1/2 cup (125g) 0% fat greek yogurt
- 1 tsp fresh thyme
- 1 egg + 2 egg whites

Preheat the oven to 375° F. Line a 9-inch pie plate with the phyllo sheet. Cook in a pan sliced zucchini with onion for 7-8 minutes. Set aside. In a large bowl combine ricotta, yogurt and thyme, then add the cooled zucchini mixture and pour onto the phyllo sheet. Bake for 35-40 minutes.

Serving size: 1 (dough+filling) Total Fat: 7 g Saturated Fat: 1.7 g Trans Fat: 0 Calories: 282 Cholesterol: 27.7 mg Protein: 10.8 g Potassium: 200 mg Carbo: 33.4 g Fiber: 2.3 g Sugar: 2. 7g Sodium: 64.5 mg

Creamy Tomato Pie

2 hours / 6 servings / Easy / Oven

Ingredients
- 1 Olive Oil Tart Crust (Dough Chapter)
- 2 pounds (900g) big tomatoes
- 1 cup (250g) low fat ricotta cheese
- 1 tbsp grated parmesan cheese
- 1 egg white
- 2 tbsp fresh chopped basil
- 2 tbsp white onion, chopped
- Pepper to taste

Preheat oven to 350° F.Coat a 9-inch removable-bottom tart pan with cooking spray and press dough into the bottom and sides of the pan. Set aside. Cut tomatoes into 1/4-inch-thick slices and remove seeds. In a bowl mix ricotta cheese with parmesan, egg white, basil, onion and pepper. Spread half of the ricotta cream on the crust, layer with half of the tomato slices, cover with ricotta cream and again tomato slices. Bake about 30-35 minutes or until golden on top.

Serving size : 1 (filling + crust) Total Fat: 13.8 g Saturated Fat: 3.8 g Trans Fat: 0 Calories: 291 Cholesterol: 17.5 mg Protein: 12.3 g Potassium: 571 mg Carbo: 29.5 g Fiber: 6.5 g Sugar: 7.3 g Sodium: 157 mg

Yummy Focaccia Pizza Margherita

1 hour / 8 servings / Super Easy / Oven

Ingredients

- 1 Italian Homemade Family Pizza Dough for Beginners (Dough Chapter)
- 1 and 1 half x 400 g can peeled tomatoes
- 2 tbsp grated parmesan cheese
- 2 tbsp extra virgin olive oil for pizza
- 2 tbsp extra virgin olive oil for sheet pan
- 1/2 pound (230gg) reduced fat mozzarella low fat soft cheese.

Take the dough out of the fridge and leave it for at least an hour so that it reaches room temperature before use. Grease a sheet pan with 2 tablespoons of extra virgin olive oil. Pour gently dough into the sheet pan and press with fingers to enlarge it. Rest for 30 minutes. Preheat oven to 550°F. Cut mozzarella into cubed pieces. Mash tomatoes with a fork. When the dough is ready cover with mashed tomatoes, spread with 2 tbsp of oil. Spread mozzarella and top and parmesan. Bake for 10-12 minutes.

Serving size: 1 (filling + dough) Total Fat: 22.5 g Saturated Fat: 7 g Trans Fat: 0 Calories: 771 Cholesterol: 19.5 mg Protein: 57.6 g Potassium: 265.5 mg Carbo: 84.5 g Fiber: 26.8 g Sugar: 0

Sodium: 254.6 mg

Creamy Broccoli and Ricotta Pie

50 mins/ 6 servings / Easy / Oven

Ingredients

- 1 Easy Flaky oil pie crust (Dough Chapter)
- 1 onion, chopped
- 7oz (500g) broccoli florets
- 1 egg
- 1/2 cup (125g) 0% fat greek yogurt
- 1 cup (240g) low-fat ricotta cheese
- 10 oz (280g) low fat minced chicken
- 1 cup (240ml) skimmed mik
- 1 tbsp cornstarch
- 2 tbsp extra virgin olive oil
- 1 tbsp grated parmesan cheese

Preheat oven to 350° F. Boil broccoli for about 5-6 minutes in water and set aside. Add in a medium saucepan oil and onion and saute for 3 minutes, than add minced chicken and let cook 3-4 minutes. Add in the saucepan with the chicken the milk and the tablespoon of cornstarch and continue to cook for other 10-12 minutes, or untill milk is absorbed. Lightly spray an 8- or 9-inch square baking dish with cooking spray. Roll out the dough to cover the baking pan, sheet must be bigger. Cover all the bottom and sides of it and let 1 inch comes out from baking pan. In a bowl mix ricotta cheese with yogurt and egg. Pour broccoli into the baking pan, add chicken, cover with ricotta mix and sprinkle with parmesan cheese. Fold the edges of the dough inside the pan, on the mix.

Bake for 25-30 minutes or until golden. Serve cool.

Serving size 1 (filling + dough) Total Fat: 33.9 g Saturated Fat: 6.9 g Trans Fat: 0 Calories: 595 Cholesterol: 46.1 mg Protein: 26.6g Potassium: 467.5 mg Carbo: 45.9 g Fiber: 7.4 g Sugar: 5.8 g Sodium: 188.5 mg

Low-Sodium Low-Fat Desserts

Low Fat Homemade Vanilla Ice Cream

30 min + freezing / 6 servings / Easy / Ice cream maker

Ingredients
- 3 tablespoons cornstarch
- 3/4 cup (150g) sugar
- 4 cups (1 Lt) skimmed milk
- 3 tsp vanilla extract
- 2 egg yolks

Combine sugar and cornstarch in a saucepan. Gradually add skimmed milk and stir until smooth. Bring to a boil over medium heat stirring for 2-3 minutes until thickened. Wisk the hot mixture little by little to egg yolks. Bring to a gentle boil again whisking constantly for 2 minutes yet. Remove for heat and add vanilla extract. Pour custard into a bowl and place it on a pan full of iced water, stirring for 2 minutes. Cover with a plastic wrap and put into the fridge.

The day after use the ice cream maker according to manufacturer's directions.

Serving size 1 Total Fat: 1.5 g Saturated Fat: 0.7 g Trans fat: 0 Calories: 187 Cholesterol: 64 mg Protein: 6.2 g Potassium: 259.7 mg Carbo: 37.3 g Fiber: 0 Sugar: 33 g Sodium: 86 mg

Healthy Pistachio and Date Raw Bites

15 min / 15 bites / Easy / Food processor

Ingredients

- 1 cup (175g) pitted whole dates
- 1/2 cup (60g) raw unsalted shelled pistachios
- 1/2 cup (50g) unsweetened shredded coconut
- 1 tsp orange extract
- 1 tsp vanilla extract

Combine dates and pistachios in a food processor and pulse until they are broken down into very little pieces.

Add coconut, orange extract and vanilla and blend until well combined. Take 1 tablespoon of mixture and make a little ball with both hands. You must have 15 pieces.

Serving size: 1 bites Total Fat: 3.2 g Saturate Fat: 1.5 g Trans Fat: 0 Calories: 57 Cholesterol: 0 Protein: 1.1 g Potassium: 21.6 mg Carbo: 6 g Fiber: 1.1 g Sugar: 4.3 g Sodium: 0.7 mg

Coconut Banana Ice Cream

15 min + freezing / 2 servings / Easy / Food processor

Ingredients

- 1 cup (230g) sliced bananas
- 2 tbsp unsweetened shredded coconut
- 1 tbsp maple syrup

Line a baking pan with parchment paper, lay banana slices with a little space between them and freeze for 6 hours. Place iced slices in a food processor and pulse until crumbly, helping you with a spatula. Add shredded coconut and syrup and blend until the mix is smooth.

Serving size: 1 Total Fat: 5 g Saturated Fat: 4.5 g Trans Fat: 0 Calories: 194 Cholesterol: 0 Protein: 1.4 g Potassium: 516.2 mg Carbo: 35.9 g Fiber: 4.8 g Sugar: 23.9 g Sodium: 4.4 mg

BlackBerries Rice Pudding

40 min / 2 servings / Easy / Saucepan

Ingredients

- 1/4 cup (50g) Arborio rice
- 2 cups (500ml) skimmed milk
- 1 tsp vanilla extract
- 1/2 cup (120g) 0% fat greek yogurt
- 1 cup (140g) frozen blackberries
- 1/2 orange, zest and juice
- 2 tsp cornflour
- 2 tsp maple syrup

Pour rice, vanilla extract and milk into a saucepan, cook over medium heat for 30 minutes, stirring occasionally. In a small saucepan add fruit, cornflour, orange zest and juice, maple syrup and cook over medium heat, stirring until it thickens. When ready, remove the rice pudding from the heat and allow to cool for 5 mins. Add yogurt to rice pudding and mix well.

Divide into 2 glasses and complete with fruit composte.

Serving size: Total Fat: 1.3 g Saturated Fat: 0 Trans Fat: 0 Calories: 304 Cholesterol: 2.7 mg Protein: 17.8 g Potassium: 102.4 mg Carbo: 55.3 g Fiber: 4.5 g Sugar: 30.9 g Sodium: 130.7 mg

Low Fat & Low Sodium Apple Pie

50 mins / 10 servings / Easy / Oven

Ingredients

- 6 big Granny Smith apples (2 & 1/2 lb - 1.2 kg),
- 4 tbsp oat flour
- 1/2 cup (100g) brown sugar
- 1 tsp cinnamon
- 1 orange zest
- 1 tsp vanilla extract
- 1 doble Pie Crust (Dough Chapter)

Preheat oven to 425° F.

Line a 9-inch pan with one of the pie crusts.

Peel apples and slice them into a bowl. Add all other ingredients, mixing well. Transfer to the crust and cover with the other dough, crimping edges together with your fingers. Make little holes with a fork and bake for 40-45 minutes, or until crust is lightly browned. Let cool well before eating.

Serving size: 1 (just filling, crust is in Dough chapter) Total Fat: 0.2 g Saturated Fat: 0 Trans Fat: 0 Calories: 100 Cholesterol: 0 Protein: 0.2 g Potassium: 0.4 mg Carbo: 24.4 g Fiber: 3.5 g Sugar: 19.8 g Sodium: 0

Low Fat Hazelnut and Pear Flan

1 hour / 6 servings / Easy / Oven

Ingredients

- 2 pears (12 oz- 350g)
- 3 tbsp whole wheat flour
- 1/4 cup (40g) ground hazelnut
- 4 tbsp granulated erythritol
- 1 egg + 2 egg whites
- 1/2 cup (120ml) skimmed milk
- 2 tbsp 0% fat greek yogurt
- 1 tsp vanilla extract
- 1 tsp orange extract

Preheat the oven to 350° F. Line a baking dish with a parcel sheet. Slice pears in equal sizes and cover the paper sheet. Whisk together egg and egg white in a bowl until well aerated. Add erythritol, hazelnut and flour slowly, spoon by spoon. Add vanilla, orange, yogurt and milk. Pour the mixture on top of the pears and place in the oven for 40 minutes.

Use a skewer to check the center of the flan. Let it cool and reverse the cake on a serving plate.

Serving size: 6 Total Fat: 5.2 g Saturated Fat: 0.7 g Trans Fat: 0 Calories: 112 Cholesterol: 31 mg Protein: 5.1 g Potassium: 96.8 mg Carbo: 11.3 g Fiber: 2.9 g Sugar: 7.2 g Sodium: 39.4 mg

Dairy-Free Iced Mocha Latte

15 min / 1 serving / Easy / Blender or Milk Frother

Ingredients

- 1/2 cup (120ml) skimmed milk
- 1/2 cup (120ml) brewed coffee or 1 espresso with water up to120 ml
- 1/2 tbsp dark cocoa powder
- 1 tsp vanilla extract
- 2 tsp maple syrup
- 2-3 ice cubes

Blend milk, coffee, cocoa, vanilla, and syrup from low to high speed for 30 seconds-1 minute. Pour the mocha latte into a big glass with ice cubes and top with a pinch of cocoa.

Serving size: 1 Total Fat: 1.1 g Saturated Fat: 0 Trans Fat:0 Calories: 94 Cholesterol: 0 Protein: 5.4 g Potassium: 88.8 mg Carbo: 15.6 g Fiber: 1g Sugar: 15 g Sodium: 55.6 mg

Dark Chocolate Pistachio Fudge Balls

15 min / 12 Balls / Easy

Ingredients

- 1/2 cup (120g) low-fat ricotta cheese
- 4 tbsp shredded, unsweetened coconut
- 1 tbsp coconut oil
- 1 tbsp granulated erythritol
- 1/2 cup (120g) shelled unsalted pistachios
- 1tsp vanilla extract
- 1 tbsp dark cocoa powder to cover

Blend coconut and coconut oil for 15-20 minutes to high speed to have coconut butter. In a bowl stir together all truffle ingredients until smooth.

Black Bean Brownies

30 min / 8 servings / Easy / Blender

Ingredients
- 3/4 cup (130g) boiled black beans
- 1/2 cup (50g) almond flour
- 1 tbsp unsweetened cocoa powder
- 1/4 cup (20g) rolled oats
- 1 egg white
- 3 tbsp maple syrup
- 2 tbsp sunflower seed oil
- 1 tsp vanilla extract
- 1 tsp baking powder
- 1/2 cup (90g) chocolate chips

Preheat oven to 350° F. Put Rolled oats in your food processor and pulse 3-4 times. Add all other ingredients, except chips, and blend until completely smooth. Add half of your chocolate chips and pour the mix into a greased 8×8 pan. Sprinkle the remaining chocolate chips over the top. Bake for 20-25 minutes.

Serving size: 1 Total Fat: 8.7 g Saturated Fat: 1.6 g Trans Fat: 0 Calories: 164 Cholesterol: 0 Protein: 4.3 g Potassium: 98.7 mg Carbo: 17.3 g Fiber: 2.6 g Sugar: 9.3 g Sodium: 72.7 mg

Freeze for 30 minutes then roll into 12 little balls with your hands and roll in the cocoa powder.

Serving size: 1 ball Total Fat: 5.7 g <u>Saturated Fat: 3.3 g</u> Trans Fat: 0 <u>Calories: 69 Cholesterol: 0</u> Protein: 2.1 g Potassium: 55.3 mg Carbo: 2.4 g Fiber: 1.3 g Sugar: 0.8 g <u>Sodium: 18.8 mg</u>

Super Easy Vanilla Banana Mug Cake

5 mins / 1 serving / Supe Easy / Microwave

Ingredients

- 6 tbsp oat flour
- 1 tbsp maple syrup
- 1 little mashed banana
- 1 tsp vanilla extract

Grease a mug. Mix all ingredients in a little bowl with a spoon and pour into the mug. Microwave 1.1/2 - 2 mins to 800 W.

Serving size: 1 Total Fat: 2.8 g <u>Saturated Fat: 0</u> Trans Fat: 0 <u>Calories: 286 Cholesterol: 0</u> Protein: 4.3 g Potassium: 463 mg Carbo: 61 g Fiber: 9 g Sugar: 26 g <u>Sodium: 3 mg</u>

Almon Vanilla Fruit Salad

25 mins / 2 servings / Easy

Ingredients

- 1/3 cup(50g) watermelon chunked
- 1/3 cup (70g) pineapple chunked
- 1/3 cup (60g) strawberries halved
- 1/3 cup (40g) apple
- 1/2 cup (120g) 0% fat greek yogurt
- 1 tbsp maple syrup
- 1 tsp vanilla extract
- 10 almonds

In a big bowl mix all fruits chopped in the same way and the halved strawberries, then divide into two serving cups. Add in a little bowl of greek yogurt, maple syrup and vanilla and mix well. Pour yogurt cream onto the fruit salad and top with almonds.

Serving size: 1 Total Fat: 3.3 g <u>Saturated Fat: 0</u> Trans Fat: 0 <u>Calories: 137 Cholesterol: 2.5 mg</u> protein: 8.2 g Potassium: 162.4 mg Carbo: 18.7 g Fiber: 1.2 g Sugar: 14.5 g <u>Sodium: 23.4 mg</u>

Low Fat Carrot Almond Cake

! Hour 30 / 6 servings /Medium

Ingredients

- 3 oz (90g) whole wheat flour
- 3 oz (90g) almond flour
- 5 oz (150g) grated carrots
- 3 oz (90g) raisins
- 2 oz (60g) brown sugar
- 2 oz (60ml) sunflower oil
- 2 egg whites
- 1/4 cup (65g) 0% fat greek yogurt
- 1 tsp each: vanilla extract, orange zest, ground cinnamon
- 2 tsp baking powder
- 2 tbsp powdered sugar

Put raisins in a glass with warm water for 30 minutes, then drain well and set aside.

Preheat oven to 325° F. Whisk brown sugar, egg whites and oil with an electric hand for 2-3 minutes.

Mix together the almond flour, whole wheat flour and baking powder. Add the wet mix to the dry one and whisk well. Add grated carrots, orange zest and raisins and whisk well together.

Pour the mix into a prepared baking pan, greased with a spray and bake for 35-40 minutes. Cake must be well-risen and firm, but soft if you lightly press it in the center.

Serve cool with powdered sugar sifted on top.

Serving size: 1 Total Fat: 17.5 g <u>Saturated Fat: 1.6 g</u> Trans Fat: 0 <u>Calories: 350 Cholesterol: 0</u> Protein: 8.4 g Potassium: 160.9 mg Carbo: 39.8 g Fiber: 4.6 g Sugar: 26.1 g <u>Sodium: 191.8 mg</u>

Low Fat Yummy Strawberry Shortcake

40 mins / 2 servings / Easy / Oven

Ingredients
- 0,4 cup (50g) whole wheat flour
- 0.4 cup (65g) 0% fat greek yogurt
- 1 tbsp granulated erythritol
- 1/2 tsp vanilla extract

Topping
- 0.4 cup (65g) 0% fat greek yogurt
- 1 tsp maple syrup
- 1/2 vanilla extract

Strawberries filling:
- 1/2 cup (70g) strawberries, diced
- 1 tsb maple syrup
- 1 tbsp water

Preheat oven to 400° F. Line a baking dish with parchment paper. Add in a bowl whole wheat flour, greek yogur, erythritol and vanilla and whisk well with a spoon. Divide with a spoon onto the baking sheet into 4 pieces and bake for 16 mins or until golden. Let them cool. Mix in a little bowl yogurt, syrup and vanilla. Set aside.

Heat a little sauce pan on low heat, strawberries diced, maple syrup and water. Cook strawberries 10-12 minutes, mashing them with a fork.

Place two shortcakes in a plate, add the yogurt cream and strawberries jam and close with the other two shortcakes.

Serving Size:1 Total Fat: 0.7 g Saturated Fat: 0 Trans Fat: 0 Calories: 110 Cholesterol: 0 Protein: 7 g Potassium: 64 mg Carbo: 18.9 g Fiber: 2.8 g Sugar: 4.1 g Sodium: 0.8 mg

Index

A
- Almon Vanilla Fruit Salad •82
- Almond flour bread rolls •41
- Anchovies Marinated in Vinegar •75
- Apple Crisp Recipe •35
- Apple-Pie Bread •31
- Artichokes and black olives Fettuccine •57
- Avocado Banana Smoothie •32

B
- Baked Tilapia with Garlic and Herbs •74
- Baked Turkey Meatballs •65
- Baked Zucchini and Potato Sticks •62
- Bamboo Piadina •40
- Banana Oats Muffin •32
- Beetroot Cutlet •62
- Berry Cheesecake Parfaits •36
- Black Bean Brownies •81
- BlackBerries Rice Pudding •79
- Blackened Cod & Tomato Basil Salade •73
- Breakfast Burrito Recipe •36
- Broccoli Cheese Soup •48
- Broiled Garlic Tilapia & Grenn Beans •71

C
- Catfish & Cherry Tomatoes Pasta •51
- Cauliflower & Peas Pasta •52
- Celery Sticks with Cream Cheese Mousse •25
- Cherry and Pistachio Yogurt Parfait •35
- Chocolate-Dipped Frozen Bananas •28
- Chocolate and Orange Muffins •32
- Chunky Vegetable Lentil Soup •46
- Coconut Banana Ice Cream •79
- Cranberry Bliss Bars •34
- Creamy Broccoli and Ricotta Pie •77
- Creamy Mushroom Soup •46
- Creamy Tofu and Turkey Salad •66
- Creamy Tomato Pie •76
- Creamy Zucchini Sauce Fusilli •52
- Crunchy Veggie Chips •26
- Curried Mushrooms and Cauliflower Soup •47

D
- Dairy-Free Chicken Pot Pie Soup •49
- Dairy-Free Iced Mocha Latte •80
- Dark Chocolate Pistachio Fudge Balls •80

E
- Easy Baked Boneless Chicken Thighs •65
- Easy Butter-Free British Dried Fruit Flapjacks •29
- Easy Flaky Oil Pie Crust (for sweet and savory filling) •42
- Easy Honey Garlic Salmon •70
- Easy Mexican Taco Turkey Meatloaf •68
- Edamame Guacamole •28
- Eggplant & Ricotta Rigatoni •56
- Eggplant & Tomato Skillet Italian-Style •60

F
- Fajita Seasoning Mix •44
- Florentine Sea Bass & Creamy Spinach •73
- Flounder Fillets & Black Olive Tomato Sauce •72
- French Toast with Strawberries •31
- Fresh Salmon Fettuccine Skillet •54
- Fresh Zucchini Pie •76

G
- Garam Masala Homemade Mix •44
- Glazed Carrot and Sweet Potato Salad •62
- Green Salad with Beets and Edamame •58

Grilled Snapper in Orange Sauce •74

Grilled Tandoori Catfish •75

H

Harvest Pumpkin Soup •46

Healthy Banana Nut Pancakes •31

Healthy Pepper Chicken Fajitas •65

Healthy Pistachio and Date Raw Bites •78

Healthy Sauteed Cabbage •61

Healthy Shrimps Spaghetti Italian Style •50

Healthy Veggie Family Meatloaf •64

Homemade Ground Turkey Burgers •66

Homemade Olive Oil Phyllo dough •41

Homemade Super Easy Oatmeal Cookies •37

I

Italian Homemade Family Wholemeal Pizza Dough •43

Italian Marinara Meatballs •68

J

Jamaican Jerk Seasoning Mix •44

L

Lemon & Ricotta Italian Frittelle •28

Lemon Baked Cod •70

Lemon Chickpea Quinoa Salade •59

Lemon Pepper Roasted Chickpeas •25

Lentil & Celery Ditalini Pasta •53

Light Oats Wholemeal Cookies •39

Low Fat & Low Sodium Apple Pie •79

Low Fat Carrot Almond Cake •82

Low Fat Hazelnut and Pear Flan •80

Low Fat Homemade Vanilla Ice Cream •78

Low Fat Yummy Strawberry Shortcake •83

Low-Fat Chicken Empanada •27

M

Mediterranean Grilled Chicken •67

O

Oatmeal Almonds and Blueberries Granola Bar •25

Olive Oil Tart Crust 9-inch pie pan recipe (no rolling pin •42

One-Pot Meat Sauce Pasta Recipe •56

Orange and Onion Chicken •69

Orange Chicken Cutle •65

Orange Low-Fat Yogurt Muffin •34

Orecchiette Pasta with Broccoli Florets •51

P

Parsley Lime Halibut Fillets •70

Peanut Butter Hummus •26

Pepper & Broccoli Chicken Pan •69

Pepper Crusted Ahi Tuna & Arugula Salad •71

Pie Crust Dough Recipe -double 9-inch pie pan recipe •41

Pumpkin Banana Bread Baked Oatmeal •37

R

Red and Yellow Bell Peppers with Zucchini •58

Red Bell Pepper Macaroni •55

Rice Flour Shortbread Dough (gluten-free/ no butter) •41

Rice Pudding with Blueberries and Figs •33

Ricotta bread rolls •41

S

Salmon Salade with Orange Vinaigrette •58

Sheet Pan Teriyaki Salmon •74

Sicilian Ricotta & Pistachios Penne Rigate •51

Southwestern Bean Salad •62

Spanakopita: a Greek Savory Pie •76

Spiced Tilapia with Tomatoes •70

Spinach & Chickpeas Lemon-spiced Chicken •69

Spinach & Ricotta Spaghetti •55

Starbucks Pumpkin Scones Copycat Recipe •38

Steak Seasoning Mix •44

Strawberry Almond Chia Pudding •35

Stuffed Pepper Soup •48

Summer Greens with Apple and Almond •60

Super Easy Vanilla Banana Mug Cake •82

Sweet Potato & Peas Lamb Chops •66

Sweet Potato and Kale Salade •61

Sweet Potato Lentil Salad •60

T

Taco Seasoning Spices Mix •44

Toast with Ricotta Cheese and Sun-Dried Tomatoes •36

Tomato & Basil Caprese Pasta Salade •53

Tomato Cucumber Salad •58

Tuna & Avocado Salade •73

Turkey Long Grain Rice Soup •48

Tuscany Panzanella Salade •63

Tuscny "Ribollita" italian recipe •45

Tzatziki Dip •25

V

Vanilla Yogurt with Peach and Pear •26

Vanilla Yogurt with Walnut and Apple •27

Veggie Potato Gateau •63

W

Walnut & Basil Penne •55

Whole wheat tortillas •40

Y

Yummy Creamy Spinach Turkey Skillet •68

Yummy Focaccia Pizza Margherita •77

No part of this publication, photos included, may be reproduced, distributed, or transmitted in any form or by any means, including photocopying, recording, or other electronic or mechanical methods, without the prior written permission of the publisher, except in the case of brief quotations embodied in critical reviews and certain other noncommercial uses permitted by copyright law.

Credits

Photo copyright (via canva.com) are owned by: ©cheche22; ©PamelaAmorimLiz; ©Rimma_Bondareko; ©smpics; ©Blueplace; ©FoodStock; ©Kcline; ©MSPhotografic; ©gbh007; ©Timolina; ©Shamtor; ©nata_vkusidey; ©Teresinagoiafoto; ©ildipapp; ©eskymaks; ©boblin; ©Kiviart; ©Kanawa_Studio; ©Superanry; ©freeskyline; ©milla1974; ©Jabiru; ©LauriPatterson; ©zkruger; ©powerofforever; ©nata_vkusidey; ©EzumeImages; ©ClaudioRampin; ©Sisoje; ©Serenacar; ©IvanNegru; ©jenifoto; ©gresei; ©Lesyy; ©AnnaLemont; ©biabaz; ©VeselovaElena; ©HausOnThePrairie; ©tashka2000; ©Robynmac; ©vm2002; ©Molka; ©SvetlanaMonyacova; ©NataBene

Printed in Great Britain
by Amazon